"The Boys" -grandsons of Perley A. Thomas- Left to Right—Albert Thomas, Pat Thomas, John W. Thomas Jr., Jim Thomas, Bill Price. In the background is a rear-engined Thomas Built Bus, The Charlotte Trolley, and a 1938 Perley A. Thomas Car Works school bus owned by the Iredell County, North Carolina School District. (John Russell Photo)

From Rails to Roads

The History of Perley A. Thomas Car Works and Thomas Built Buses

by Clint Johnson

Cover: color photograph by John Russell, B&W photograph courtesy of High Point Museum collection

THIS IS A LIFESCAPES CORPORATE BIOGRAPHY

Published in 1996 by Lifescapes Corporation

Printed in the United States of America

ISBN 1-886701-04-0

Library of Congress Catalog Card Number 95-81897

Lifescapes Corporation
2418 Blue Ridge Road
Suite 208
Raleigh, NC 27607
(919) 571-0944

CONTENTS

Dedication

This history of Perley A. Thomas Car Works and Thomas Built Buses is dedicated to the thousands of people who have worked for and with the company for 80 years.

While Mr. P.A. had the vision for the company, it was the men and women working in the offices and factories who made his dreams realities. We thank all of you for your contributions.

– The Thomas Family

ACKNOWLEDGMENTS

This book was made possible by a number of people including the following who sat around a dining room table talking about the founding of their company:

Norman Thomas of High Point, son of Perley A. Thomas
Jim Thomas of High Point, Norman's son
Bill Price of High Point, Melva Thomas Price's son
John W. Thomas, Jr. of High Point, Willard's son
Pat Thomas of High Point, Willard's son
Albert L. Thomas, Norman's son

Thanks also go to:

R. Wesley Bender of Springfield, Iowa who provided most of the reference material on the history of streetcars and photos of the Perley A. Thomas car that still runs in Mt. Pleasant, Iowa at the Midwest Old Threshers Reunion. His enthusiasm for streetcars is proof that there are thousands of people in the country who still revere the name Perley A. Thomas.

Chris Allen of Charlotte Trolley in Charlotte, N.C. for providing the names of streetcar enthusiasts around the country, and for opening the museum several times for photo sessions and research visits.

Tom Bolan of Hannibal, Missouri for passing along R. Wesley Bender's name.

Joe Bell of Knoxville, Tenn. who provided some of the photos used in the book.

William Middleton, author of *The Time of the Trolley*, for providing photos from his private collection.

George Sanborn of the Massachusetts State Transportation Library for his suggestions and as a source of reference material.

Fred Perry of the Seashore Trolley Museum in Kennebunkport, Maine for providing a list of names of people who love Perley A. Thomas Car Works streetcars.

The librarians of the High Point City Library for digging up source material.

The High Point Historical Museum for allowing us to rephotograph the photo of Perley A. Thomas Car Works workers assembling streetcars.

John Russell, High Point photographer, for taking original photos and reproducing some old family photos.

FOREWORD

Most company histories have a very limited readership, composed primarily of employees and shareholders. This volume deserves a much wider audience for several reasons. First, it is well-written and thoroughly researched. Furthermore, it chronicles not just a company, but also the remarkable Thomas family, which is now in its fourth generation of leadership of what is now called Thomas Built Buses.

The primary reason I hope it is read by many who are not affiliated with the company is the message it conveys about the American dream. Perley A. Thomas was a visionary who would not be deterred by any obstacle. He was determined to build mass transportation vehicles of high quality, and he did so. Two world wars, a depression, the evaporation of the streetcar market, a plant fire—all of these became challenges to be met rather than reasons to give up. As a result of his drive and marketing, manufacturing and designing skills, as well as the similar qualities in those who have led the company in later years, Thomas Built Buses are in use by the hundreds of thousands all over the world. Equally noteworthy is that streetcars built seventy years ago by Perley A. Thomas Car Works are in regular service today in New Orleans.

This book describes a company and its people who continue to look for new markets, both geographically and in terms of new products. They also carry on the legacy of the founder with their strong interest in continuously improving the safety features of their buses. Perley A. Thomas was emphasizing safety several decades before the federal government started regulating the safety features of buses. You will read here of his creation in the 1930s of a much safer design for the bus body frame. Recently, his successors introduced a child safety seat specifically designed to work with bus seats.

They are now filling the largest order in the company's history, 2,000 state-of-the-art, transit-type school buses to be used by the school children of South Carolina. The flat nose cab design makes it easier for the driver to see small children crossing in front of the bus.

Since it was founded in 1916, the company has been based in High Point, North Carolina. Its success in the 80 years since Perley A. Thomas used $6,000 borrowed from a bank, along with $700 his wife had inherited, to buy its original equipment is a tribute to the thousands of dedicated employees over the years who have built the streetcars and buses. Both the Canadian and U.S. factories have been staffed with people who share the Thomas family's dedication to quality.

I grew up in High Point, and I have been privileged to know since childhood quite a few members of the Thomas family and many of their employees. I thought of them on a hot day in the summer of 1988 when I participated in the ceremonies inaugurating service on the New Orleans Riverfront line by streetcars known as "The Ladies In Red" (i.e., restored Perley A. Thomas Series 900 cars). As I have traveled in many areas of the world on business and for pleasure, on countless occasions I have seen the Thomas Built Buses logo thousands of miles away from my hometown. Whenever I see it, I think of old friends who had a hand in building the bus on which it appears; and my chest swells a little with civic pride.

If the vehicle in question is a school bus, I also think of the parents of the children who ride on it. Whether those parents know it or not, their children are a lot safer because of the efforts of the people described in this book. As a parent whose children have ridden safely on Thomas Built buses, I want to say thank you to the company and its people. You justly deserve to have your story told and preserved, as is so well done in the pages that follow.

– James H. Burnley IV

James H. Burnley IV

Jim Burnley, a native of High Point, is a former Secretary of the U.S. Department of Transportation.

Prior to serving as Secretary, Mr. Burnley was General Counsel of the Department in 1983 and then Deputy Secretary through 1987. He played a key role in the $1.7 billion public offering of Conrail as well as in numerous aviation, automobile and other transportation regulatory matters. He joined the Transportation Department after serving as Associate Deputy Attorney General at the Department of Justice.

He now practices law in Washington, specializing in federal regulatory matters. He serves on the boards of several charitable and educational foundations, and he remains active in national politics.

Mr. Burnley received his undergraduate degree from Yale University and his law degree from Harvard Law School.

INTRODUCTION

The descendants of the industrial entrepreneurs of the early part of the 20th century usually cannot see what their ancestors contributed to the country's growth. At best, the inventions or machines designed by their forebears are statically displayed in a museum. At worst, they are lost to history, described only by notes scrawled in great-grandfather's notebook.

That is not so with the descendants of Perley A. Thomas of High Point, North Carolina. His family can see what Thomas contributed to the world. His products are still in use.

Streetcars Thomas designed in 1923 are used every day in New Orleans, Louisiana, by thousands of commuters. Another runs at a streetcar museum in Kennebunkport, Maine. Still another operates at a hotel in Chattanooga, Tenn. A streetcar Thomas designed in 1929 runs on holiday weekends in Mount Pleasant, Iowa.

Streetcars are not the only Thomas-designed vehicles still operating. A 1938 Thomas school bus bought by the Iredell County, North Carolina, school system is still in perfect running condition.

The Thomas family knows that these products are special tributes to the talents possessed by a man they always called "Mr. P.A."

It is rare that a working example of an ancestor's mechanical contribution to society can be found because few people use old machines on a daily basis. Take the telephone, for instance. Alexander Graham Bell's first crude telephone was quickly replaced by better technology he developed. Telephones today bear little resemblance to Bell's original invention. It is doubtful that Bell would even recognize the latest version of his device. Certainly, no one today uses Bell's original telephones.

The Wright Brothers invented the airplane. But the balsa wood and fabric flying machine created by the brothers now hangs from the ceiling of a museum, never to fly again. It is too small, too fragile, too dangerous to be flown by anyone.

Tom Watson, who kept a "Think" sign over his desk, founded the International Business Machines Corporation. Today's IBM managers would be astonished if their customers were still using Watson's early office machines. Watson's descendants have to be satisfied with reading books about his role in making IBM office machines the world's standard.

The children, grandchildren, great-grandchildren and great-great-grandchildren of Perley A. Thomas are different from the families of those pioneering entrepreneurs. The Thomas family can still experience what Mr. P.A. created in his factory on Commerce Street in High Point, North Carolina. They can see, touch and ride in streetcars designed and manufactured by him. They can ride in a 55-year-old school bus that runs as good today as the day it left the assembly line.

The legacy of Perley A. Thomas goes well beyond the ability of his family to ride in antique streetcars and school buses. His lasting gift to his family—and the nation—was a company charged with the daily transportation of millions of people over uncounted thousands of miles of roads. Founded in 1916 as the Perley A. Thomas Car Works, the company today is called Thomas Built Buses.

The reason behind the continuing success of Thomas Built Buses is simple. The man who was always pursuing new design challenges discovered in 1936 that the State of North Carolina needed more school buses. He went after the contract though he had little experience in automotive design, bus manufacturing, or automobile mechanics. It is doubtful he had even been inside a school bus before he made a bid to manufacture them.

Inexperience in manufacturing buses did not stop Thomas or his sons and daughter, Willard, Norman and Melva, from submitting a bid. They urgently needed a new product to carry the company into the future. If they won the bid, buses would be that new product. If they lost . . . well, no one will ever know what would have happened.

They won the bid. Perley A. Thomas Car Works, a respected manufacturer of streetcars, transformed itself into a manufacturer of buses. It continues in that business today under the corporate name of Thomas Built Buses, a manufacturer of a wide-ranging product line of school buses, transit buses, and specialty buses.

In 1995, Thomas Built Buses is the world's largest manufacturer of school buses. More than 300,000 Thomas Built buses have rolled off assembly lines in the United States, Canada, Ecuador, Mexico and Peru since Mr. P. A. won his first school bus bid in 1936. They have been assembled in seven other countries in temporary facilities to comply with bids. Thomas Built buses have been sold in every state of the nation, in every province of Canada, in nearly every country of South America, in most of the Middle East nations, and in other far flung corners of the world.

At the main plant in High Point, North Carolina, on the same site where streetcars were once rolled onto railroad flatcars, 36 buses per day come off the assembly line. With more than 1,000 employees, Thomas Built Buses is one of the largest employers in Guilford County and the largest industrial manufacturer in High Point.

Always an innovator, Thomas Built Buses is planning for the future by developing school buses that run on alternative fuels such as natural gas and electricity. The company is regularly developing new safety devices to protect the millions of passengers who use its buses every day.

All this started when a nattily-dressed, self-taught, Canadian-born, mechanical engineer decided to take a job offer with a company he did not know in a small North Carolina town he never knew existed.

CHAPTER 1

A Canadian in The States

Family members suppose Perley (pronounced "PEARL-e") A. Thomas inherited his ability to design mechanical devices and work with wood from his father, John A. Thomas. John was born in 1846 on a farm near the town of Chatham, in the Canadian province of Ontario. Little more is known of John, other than that he was of Welsh stock and that he married Margaret Cunningham, another Canadian of English descent born in 1850.

The union of John and Margaret produced nine children over the course of 18 years. The second-born was Perley A., who arrived on September 11, 1874, just a year and a half after his oldest brother, George. Later, sisters Mabel, Louise, Maude, Caroline and Rose would join twins Alex and Grace.

Perley's early life was spent on the farm where he learned from his father how to repair machinery. John was a millwright, a 19th century version of a mechanic, who traveled between factories installing and maintaining equipment. Millwrights rarely specialized in types of industries or even types of equipment. If the machinery had gears and belts and ran on coal or wood, millwrights learned how to fix it. That sort of skill would serve Perley well in years to come.

At the same time that Perley was learning to work with steel machinery, he was also developing a lifelong fascination with woodworking. As a teenager he began to collect hammers, chisels, and wood vises that he used to craft chests of drawers, tables, chairs and fireplace mantels for neighbors. For the rest of his life, his box of woodworking tools would be by his side.

On a neighboring farm was the Scotch-descended Milne family. By coincidence, the parents of this family were also named John and Margaret. Like the Thomas family, the Milne family was large with four boys and five girls. Among them was Margaret, born on September 28, 1875, just over a year younger than Perley.

Thomas family legend has it that one of Perley's sisters was best friends with Margaret, which must have put her in frequent and close contact with the budding farm mechanic. Whatever the circumstances, they were childhood sweethearts. They married in 1896.

The late 19th century was an exciting era for men with mechanical and design skills. It must have seemed that everything important was being invented and improved all at the same time. Electricity was replacing gas as a means of lighting. Telephones were being installed in homes and businesses. Perhaps the most important invention of the period was the automobile. Many manufacturers were trying their hands at it, including some in the bustling industrial city of Detroit, just 50 miles from Chatham.

The demand for skilled mechanics was probably one of the lures that attracted the Thomas family. Perley, his wife Margaret and their two children, Melva, born in 1898, and Willard, born in 1900, immigrated from Canada to Detroit in 1901.

Perley A. Thomas from a painting hanging in the home of Norman Thomas

Margaret Milne Thomas from a painting hanging in the home of Norman Thomas

Lack of a formal engineering education was no deterrent to finding a design job. Despite the fact he had only finished the fourth grade in Canada, Thomas was able to demonstrate his knowledge of how things worked and how to make them work better.

Although he was in the birthplace of the auto industry, Thomas was originally attracted to his first love, woodworking. He found a job designing hulls for a yacht company. Family history does not record how a farm boy knew anything about boats. That must have become apparent to him or his employer rather quickly, because he soon left the yacht company and started a life's career in mass transit. His second job was as a design engineer with the streetcar division of the Detroit United Railroad.

The family stayed in Detroit only three years, long enough for second son Norman to be born June 27, 1903. By 1906 Thomas was working with the Kuhlman Car Company of Cleveland, a subsidiary of the J.G. Brill Company of Philadelphia, the nation's leading trolley manufacturer. ("Trolley" and "streetcar" are synonymous in most cities with the exception of New Orleans. In that city the only acceptable term is "streetcar.")

While working for Kuhlman, Thomas decided that his fourth grade education and self-taught engineering design skills would carry him only so far in the emerging corporate structure at the turn of the century. He started attending Case Institute of Technology at night to pursue a structural engineering degree. While there he exhibited a brashness and confidence in his own engineering abilities that would mark his character to his dying day. This self-assurance would help him start his own company within 10 years.

Family legend says that Thomas once challenged a bridge design being promoted as an example of good engineering by one of the school's professors. Thomas, the grade school dropout and night school engineering student, had the nerve to tell the college professor that the bridge's superstructure would not hold up under load and severe weather conditions. The bridge collapsed years after it was built—just as Thomas had predicted it would.

While working for Kuhlman in 1910, Thomas met two men who worked for Stone & Webster Engineering Company of Boston, a public utilities holding company that was active in the streetcar industry. They told him about an opening for chief engineer with a growing streetcar manufacturer called the Southern Car Company in the tiny North Carolina town of High Point.

The Stone & Webster men must have been very persuasive salesmen, both to Thomas and to the executives of Southern Car Company. Thomas applied for the job without ever visiting the factory or the town. He was hired without even interviewing for it in person. According to family history, all negotiations for the job were conducted by letter, telephone and telegram.

The Thomas family's decision to move to High Point was partially made by wife Margaret. At the same time the offer from Southern Car Company was made, Thomas had also received a second offer to join the Cincinnati Car Company. Margaret, a native of cold Canada who had grown tired of heavy winter snows in Cleveland, thought the picturesque-sounding town of High Point (named for the highest point on the railroad line between Greensboro and Charlotte) would be much warmer. She told Perley that he should take the High Point job.

What Margaret had not counted on, however, was that rural North Carolina in 1910 was nothing like urban Cleveland. While riding the train into the state, she began to have misgivings when she saw miles of red clay but no major cities. She was also upset to discover that Catholic Church services were held only once a month because the denomination counted only a few thousand followers in the entire state.

Although she probably missed the big city advantages she lost by moving to a small town, Margaret soon adapted and made herself at home. In 1916, at age 42, she had one more child, a daughter named Mary Elizabeth. Mary was the only one of the four children of Perley A. and Margaret Thomas who was born a native of High Point.

Mrs. Margaret Milne Thomas, wife of P.A. Thomas with her four children (circa 1950). From left to right—older son, Willard; Margaret Milne Thomas; older daughter, Melva; younger daughter, Mary; and younger son, Norman.

When Thomas joined Southern Car Company in 1910, it was already a successful trolley manufacturer with a reputation for building lightweight, wooden streetcars. Organized by executives from The Briggs Car Company of Amesbury, Massachusetts, the company claimed in advertisements that it had moved to North Carolina to take advantage of "the best timber section of the South." Originally formed in 1890, Briggs Car Company had built streetcars for many towns and cities in New England before the Massachusetts plant was closed in 1903 and the production equipment moved south to High Point.

Because North Carolina had no history of streetcar manufacturing, the Southern Car Company's 1904 advertisements assured potential customers that executives had also retained "the services of the skilled car builders from the North." That statement was supposed to convince customers as far away as New York City and Puerto Rico that the quality they expected from a Massachusetts company would be continued in North Carolina.

Within two years after Thomas had joined the company in 1910, Southern had sold streetcars in 17 states and at least one foreign country. Southern Car Company streetcars traveled the rails in such large cities as New York, Chicago and New Orleans. One of its early cars was an elegant machine the company called "Merrymaking." Riders could sit inside, or on a mild day, lounge in wicker chairs on an open platform.

The Thomas family believes that one of the reasons Mr. P.A. was hired—sight unseen—was his skill in making wood do what he wanted it to do. Woodworking was an important craft in the early 1900's when most streetcar bodies and interior support beams were still made of wood. Mr. P.A. knew what woods were best for the strength necessary to support the weight of passengers, and what woods provided the most attractive interior paneling.

He was an artist in woodworking. He even made his own wooden drafting tools such as T-squares and engineering scales with measurements graded down to 1/64th of an inch. (These tools are now prized possessions of the Thomas family.)

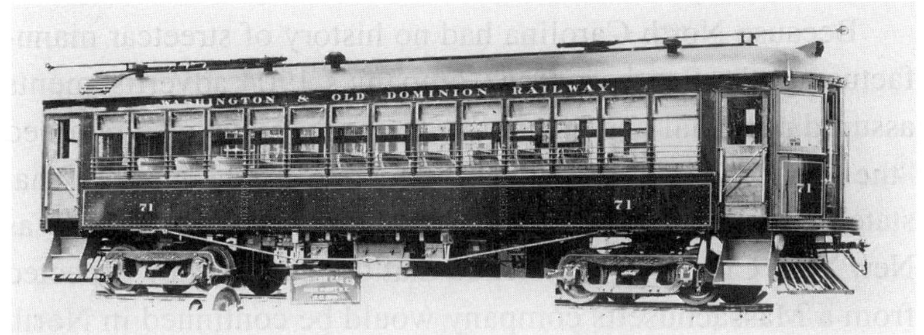

Washington & Old Dominion Railway Interurban Car No. 106 built by Southern Car Company. (William D. Middleton photo collection)

Long Island Traction Company Car No. 67 built by Southern Car Company. (William D. Middleton photo collection)

Within five years of his hiring, the industry began to move to all-steel streetcar construction and Mr. P.A. did not skip a beat. Southern Car Company produced streetcars for transit systems all along the Eastern seaboard, including 11 streetcars for the Philadelphia and Western Railway. In 1913, Southern Car Company delivered 10 streetcars that ran in Washington, D.C. Mr. P.A. may have designed one of the most interesting looking machines in streetcar history, Car 1000, a double-decked, all-steel car that was originally intended for sight-seeing in Washington. It was used for nearly four years, but was finally converted to a single-decked car. In 1915, New Orleans purchased 52 of Southern Car Company's 400-series cars designed by Thomas. The cars were of all steel construction, seated 52 people, and cost $3,000 each.

Despite its successes in selling streetcars, the Southern Car Company could not compete with larger operations such as the J.G. Brill Company of Philadelphia and St. Louis Car Company, the two giants of their day. Management tried bringing in A.H. Sisson, a management veteran of competitive streetcar manufacturers like the St. Louis Car Company and Forsyth Brothers Company of Chicago. Even Mr. Sisson could not turn the company into a growing concern. By 1916, the Southern Car Company was out of business, its skilled woodworkers forced to take jobs with the lower paying furniture factories in High Point.

Thomas refused to take a simple factory job. He was a skilled woodworker who had designed furniture since he was a teenager. Instead of hiring on at one of the local furniture factories, he became one of the region's skilled wood craftsmen, starting his own one-man business called the High Point Mantel Company. He built chairs, tables, cabinets and specialized in residential fireplace mantels made from exotic woods such as cherry and mahogany. When his residential business was slack, he called on businesses and churches. Some churches in High Point still use altars built by Thomas in 1916.

Mr. P.A.'s (he acquired the nickname at some point after starting his own company) teenaged sons, Willard and Norman, did what they could to help make ends meet. Both took jobs sanding and sawing in local furniture factories. Sometimes they heard the snickers of other employees, who knew their father had been chief engineer for the bankrupt streetcar company. The boys never answered the taunts because they had faith in their father.

In the summer of 1916, the Southern Public Utilities Company in Charlotte, North Carolina—a forerunner of today's utilities giant Duke Power Company—contacted Thomas with the offer of a one-time renovation job on some of its Southern Car Company streetcars.

Early streetcar manufacturing practice called for two styles of cars: open for summer use and closed for winter. Open streetcars in the south had no windows or even sides so summer breezes could help cool passengers. Rain was kept out, at least in theory, by dropping canvas along the streetcar's side. More expensive winter streetcars had sides and windows. As the weather grew colder, summer streetcars were simply stored until spring.

The Southern Public Utilities transit officials saw the inefficiency of keeping its summer streetcars idle for almost a third of the year. They contacted Thomas with a proposal and a budget that would allow him to gather a crew of former Southern Car Company employees to enclose them. The transit company had considered having its own employees do the work, but because Thomas had designed the cars and Southern Car Company employees had built them, it made more sense to subcontract the work.

Thomas put together the crew and sent them to Charlotte. Mr. P.A. himself remained in High Point to develop a marketing plan he would take to a local bank. He reasoned that if Charlotte's utility company wanted to convert its summer streetcars to year-round streetcars, there must be hundreds, perhaps thousands of other streetcars around the country that could also be converted. He recognized an opportunity when one presented itself.

Thomas wrote letters and visited cities with streetcar systems. He made special calls on towns located close to U.S. Army bases and military contractors. He realized that the United States' eventual entry into the First World War would create a demand for safe, reliable, year-round transportation to and from military installations. That meant streetcars.

Within a few months of the failure of the Southern Car Company, its chief engineer had invested $6,000 in bank funds and $700 from his wife's inheritance in a new company. He purchased his old employer's manufacturing equipment at a bankruptcy auction and bought the closed Sunnyside Ice Company building for a new factory. He then tracked down and hired many of Southern's former employees. In April 1917 Perley A. Thomas Car Works had an order in hand to deliver nine renovated, enclosed street cars to the U.S. Navy shipyard in Mobile.

Willard and Norman immediately quit their furniture factory jobs and joined their father in what would become one of High Point, North Carolina's most successful family businesses.

Chapter 2

Streetcars—the Most Efficient Transportation Ever Invented

To understand the impact that Perley A. Thomas and his company had on transportation in the country, it is necessary to examine the history, development and workings of the streetcar. In short, streetcars such as those designed by men like Mr. P.A. were in large part responsible for today's municipal mass transit systems. Beyond that direct impact, streetcars also played a role in the development of the suburbs and amusement parks.

The late teens and the 1920's were exciting times for electric streetcar manufacturers. It was an industry booming with orders and teeming with competitors. Like most industries, it could trace its roots back to a single man. That man was a person who revolutionized the mass transit industry, but who modestly neglected to legally tie his name to his inventions.

He was Frank J. Sprague. Born in Connecticut in 1857, Sprague showed early signs that he would be no ordinary man. Sprague entered the U.S. Naval Academy and graduated at age 20 in 1878. Reaching shore after his first long cruise, he promptly filed more than 60 electrical patents. In 1882 he attended the Crystal Palace Exhibition in London. It was there that he developed the idea of an electric trolley to replace the coal-burning locomotives that were then pulling passenger cars in the underground subways. Watching people choking in the smoke-filled tunnels, he knew there had to be a better means of transportation.

Developing an electric trolley was Sprague's consuming interest. To finance his dream, he started designing electric motors. Sprague's designs were so good that Thomas Edison endorsed them.

By 1886 Sprague had made enough money from selling his motors that he was ready to start work on his trolley. He started experimenting with a flat car powered by electric motors fed by electricity running from overhead lines. In 1887 he signed a $110,000 contract to introduce a streetcar system on the streets of Richmond, Virginia.

Sprague found it difficult to make his electric trolleys work, particularly up Richmond's steep hills. Once he was forced to hire a team of horses to move a streetcar that had stopped dead on the tracks. It took more than a year to make the electric trolleys run reliably. Sprague estimated that he spent $185,000, $75,000 more than he was paid by the city of Richmond, but the streetcars finally did transport passengers as he had promised they would.

Within a year of the opening of Richmond's electric streetcar line, there were 200 other systems operating or under construction in cities around the country. More than half of the systems were equipped by Sprague's company and almost all of them were using his patents. The electric streetcar industry would forever change the way American cities would work and grow.

Although his name association with trolleys has long since been forgotten by everyone but railway historians, Sprague's electric streetcar was the perfect urban vehicle. Horses, which had powered trolleys for years, presented problems because of the urine and manure they left behind to be flushed into the city's drainage systems. The streetcar consumed only electricity and excreted nothing. The electric trolley carried more than twice as many passengers as a horsecar could manage. It traveled the same rails that had originally been laid for the horsecars, so infrastructure up-fitting was minor. It could move faster than a horsedrawn streetcar. Best of all, the electric streetcar used the same electric lines that were already in place to service the city's business and residential districts.

The electric streetcar traveled from where the people lived in trolley suburbs to the large buildings where they worked downtown. For most city dwellers, there was no need to own an automobile. Fares were affordable. Fares in High Point, North Carolina, were a nickel, which included a transfer. One famous New York City trolley using two Perley A. Thomas streetcars was called The Three Penny Line. New Orleans riders could ride to Carrollton, almost 14 miles away, for a quarter.

The appeal of trolleys, even in the emerging age of the automobile was obvious. The streetcar fare was only pennies a day. Why spend a fortune buying an expensive car that required hand cranking, ran on explosive gasoline, and which transferred every bump in the road through the rock solid suspension into the bones and muscles of the owner?

Riding the trolley was the way to move around the city! Nearly every citizen agreed. One survey of 1917 trolley usage shows streetcars operating in the United States moved 11 billion passengers a year along 45,000 miles of track. Ridership peaked around 28 billion passengers a year in the late 1920's. (The survey counts each boarding as one passenger so a person changing cars to and from work counted as several passengers each day.)

Trolley suburbs became common in many cities as successful business executives bought houses miles away from the urban bustle. To increase their weekend business when many office and factory workers would not be riding, some trolley companies built amusement parks at the end of the line. As cities grew, the utility companies that operated the lines simply added more streetcars. Estimates are that more than 100,000 electric streetcars were manufactured and put in service over the course of 50 years.

Manufacturers were scattered all over the country. The largest was the J.G. Brill Car Company of Philadelphia, which not only manufactured streetcars, but also supplied many other manufacturers with the "single-truck" or "double truck" running wheels. (A double truck is a double set of wheels under each end of the streetcar.) According to Thomas family estimates, Brill may have had up to one half of the market at one time, followed in size by the St. Louis Car Company, which had up to 20 percent of the market, then the Cincinnati Car Company with 15 percent of the market. The Perley A. Thomas Car Works was probably the fourth largest streetcar manufacturer with five percent of the market at the company's peak in 1924. After Perley A. Thomas Car Works came a number of smaller, regional manufacturers. Some city transit companies built and repaired their own trolleys by buying parts from the traditional manufacturers.

Trolleys were simple, efficient machines, which played a large role in increasing their popularity among municipal transportation companies.

The average streetcar capacity was between 40 and 52 people. It was usually between 39 and 48 feet long. The wheels were 26 to 33 inches in diameter. Under the floor at each end of the car were either one or two electric motors to drive the wheels. The motors were usually rated between 35 and 60 horsepower each. The empty cars weighed between 30,000 and 33,000 pounds.

Most cars had two poles mounted on their roofs. Power to the car was supplied at approximately 600 volts direct current from the electric substation through the main breaker to the trolley wire 19 feet above the ground. The electricity was then picked up by the trolley wheel (or "harp"), carried down the pole through the circuit breaker, to the controller through "resistor grids" to the motors. The power returned through the wheels to the rails and back to the substation to complete the circuit.

The trailing pole always powered the trolley and the front pole was hooked down on the roof to eliminate any potential problem with hitting a wire kink or a curve that might bend and break the pole.

Streetcar systems were designed one of two ways: with a turnaround at the end of the line at which the car would make a U-turn to head in the opposite direction, or a dead-end. When the trolley reached the end of the line and there was no turnaround, the motorman would stop and reverse the seat backs so the passengers would be facing forward on the return trip. After switching the seats, he got out and untied the front pole to engage the wire. He then walked back and tied down the formerly active rear pole and climbed in what had been the back of the car. He picked up his controller handles and moved forward to start the return trip. Power controls were usually at both ends of the streetcar, unless the city planned only u-turns on its streetcar systems.

A motorman had to be trained in the nature of electricity and how it reacts with electric motors. Electric motors have a low resistance when starting. Resistance increases as the speed increases so the flow of current had to be limited when first applied to prevent burning out the motor windings.

The motorman stood at a "controller," which rotated clockwise through successive notches. Each notch governed the amount of electricity being fed to the motors. Going through the notches was much like shifting gears in a truck. If the highest notch was reached, each motor received full current. At that point, the car would be at its maximum speed, a rated 28 mph with the 900 series Thomas Car Works cars now in use in New Orleans, which have 65 horsepower motors. Mr. P.A. liked to install powerful motors in his streetcars.

Stopping power was supplied by compressed air brakes powered by the same electric line. Each trolley had a 600-volt direct current air compressor mounted under the carriage that supplied air to reservoir tanks. Every morning before the first run, the motorman would untie the power pole and allow the compressor a few minutes to store air in its tanks before he would start on the streets.

The brakes themselves were simple. When a stop was to be made, the motorman would move the brake handle slowly and steadily to apply air to the brake cylinder. He would use his judgment to supply enough air to stop the car smoothly then he would return the handle to its center position.

While steering the streetcar was obviously not a problem since the car always followed the rails, it took a skilled motorman to bring the car up to speed without jerking the passengers backward and even more skill to stop the car smoothly without throwing the passengers forward. Just as with railroad trains today, braking a streetcar took time. The motorman's responsibilities were to the safety of his passengers so pedestrians or motorists pulling in front of a streetcar risked their lives if they thought the motorman could or would always stop.

Urban dwellers today are accustomed to hearing idling and racing automotive engines. A streetcar was almost silent in its operation. In the morning, the first sound a motorman heard was the pumping up of the air compressor once he engaged the pole to the line. When he engaged the electric motors, there was almost no sound, except for the clicking of the wheels and the grinding of the gears. The silence of the streetcar's operation was one of the reasons for installing a loud, distinctive bell. The bell was usually operated by a foot pedal and would be used by the motorman to warn unaware pedestrians and to announce upcoming trolley stops. If pedestrians or the occasional vehicle still did not acknowledge the trolley's presence and get out of the way, a steel bumper and a net-like "people catcher" on each end shoved them from under the streetcar's unforgiving steel wheels.

Perley A. Thomas never spent much time worrying about his larger manufacturing competitors. He was confident in his own engineering. One Thomas family story says that a competitor made a point of telling its customers that every one of its cars was tested for resistance to high voltage before leaving the factory. According to Thomas family legend, during one of those tests, at least two completed cars overheated and caught fire. Perley A. Thomas Car Works never tested its cars before they left the factory, but no Thomas car failed or caught fire due to electrical failure.

Streetcar manufacturers boasted of repeat orders. In 1914, the Southern Car Company ran an ad showing individual pictures of nine different models it had built for nine cities that year. The ad copy read: "There are three requisites for a man's success; honesty, education and thrift. These same requisites can be applied to the success of a manufacturing institution. HONESTY to cover good workmanship and materials; EDUCATION to cover versatility of construction and THRIFT to get the business. Our honesty is proven by our duplicate orders; our education is proven by the different types of cars that we have constructed; our thrift is proven by the record we have made by not having our plant closed a single day for the past two years for want of orders. Let us have your specifications and inquiries."

Perley A. Thomas Car Works was ready to follow the same marketing strategy.

CHAPTER 3

Perley A. Thomas Car Works Is Born

While the coming of World War I gave Perley A. Thomas Car Works its big economic boost, it also slowed the company's growth for a couple of years because the federal government restricted the construction of new municipal streetcars. All streetcar renovations and construction were aimed at helping the war effort. One source says that only 100 street cars were manufactured during the U.S. involvement in World War I and most of them were used to transport workers to the Philadelphia Shipyard.

Once the War was over and millions of soldiers were returning home to jobs they hoped to find in the growing cities, there was a pent-up demand for mass transit. Thomas was in a good position to catch this wave of growth. Attracted by Mr. P.A.'s considerable reputation as chief engineer for Southern Car Company, transit companies had no qualms about ordering streetcars from the new Perley A.Thomas Car Works.

Oddly enough, the city of High Point was not the first to order streetcars from its new hometown company. That honor fell to the city of Winston-Salem, 25 miles away, which ordered two streetcars in 1918 at a cost of around $4,000 each.

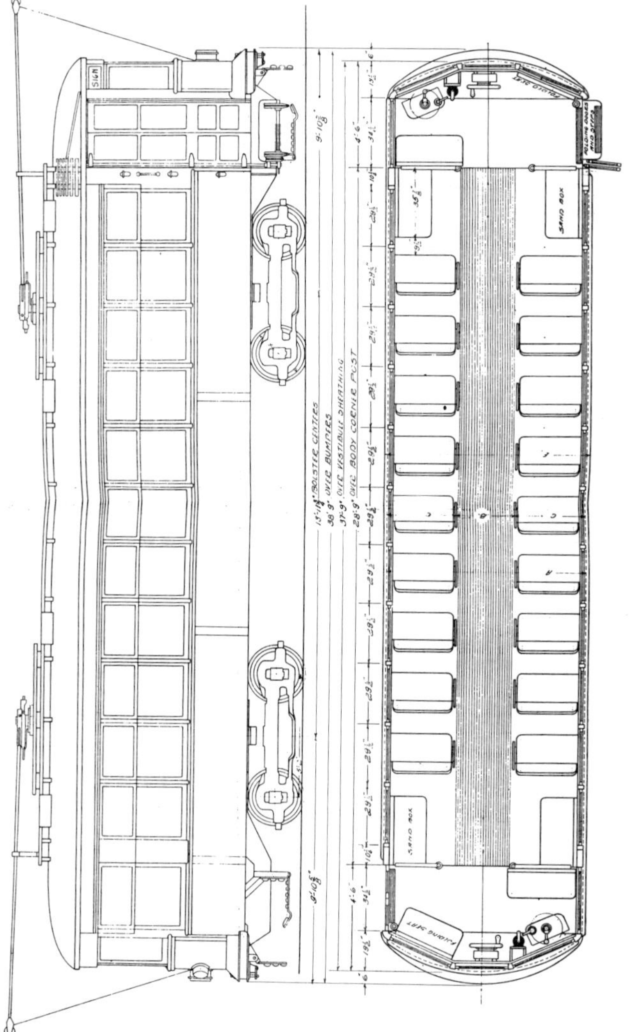

Drawing of an unidentified Perley A. Thomas street car featuring left-hand drive and a folding seat at each end for the toll collector. Note the sandbox at each end. Sand would be released on the rails when needed to help secure traction.

Winston-Salem's order was followed closely by New York City, which needed two new streetcars for its Three Penny Line that ran over the Manhattan Bridge. High Point may have been the company's third customer.

As the orders mounted, the surging growth for Perley A. Thomas Car Works provided the opportunity for oldest son Willard to come work for his father full-time.

Willard had first worked for the company on the renovation of the Charlotte cars, acting as a 17-year-old courier of the payroll between High Point and Charlotte. Norman, two years younger, was still working part time in a furniture factory, waiting for his opportunity to come work for his father. Moving to a streetcar factory could not come too soon for him.

On Norman's first summer day working in the hot furniture factory, he wore a short-sleeved shirt. The other factory workers just grinned at the inexperienced Yankee kid. By the end of his shift Norman's arms were scratched, full of splinters and bleeding from the repeated bumping they took as the boards worked their way through a planer. It was then he noticed that everyone else wore long-sleeved shirts and that many of his fellow workers were missing one or more digits from one or both hands. When he saw some former furniture workers missing arms from their carelessness around huge power saws, Norman was convinced that his future also lay with his father's streetcar company.

Streetcar orders were soon coming in from all over the southeastern United States and even the Caribbean. It was a 12-car purchase by the growing city of Miami that showed the lengths Mr. P.A. would go to service his customers. Once the streetcars were received in Miami, their operators discovered that a fist-sized door opening mechanism had been inadvertently left off one of the units. Norman Thomas took a train from High Point to Charlotte, N.C., and another nonstop train

A young Willard Thomas holds his son, John W. Thomas Jr. (1927).

Inside the Perley A. Thomas Car Works factory. Five streetcars can be seen. There was room for at least 15 under one roof. These appear to be early models, indicating the photo may have been taken as early as 1917 or 1918. The factory's roof has skylights.

from Charlotte to Miami to personally install the missing door opener. Norman did not take any vacation time to enjoy the sunshine and the beach. Within an hour after arriving in Miami, he had finished the installation and was waiting in the station for the next train north so he could return to manufacturing more streetcars. Mr. P.A. would have it no other way.

At least four Thomas streetcars were sold in San Juan, Puerto Rico, with left-hand drive instead of the traditional center drive. Thomas followed the customer's instructions that the doors remain small because, in the transit manager's words, "passengers don't mind shoving each other to get on the streetcar." One streetcar was sold to a line in Havana, Cuba.

Perley A. Thomas shipped as far west as Montana. The Anaconda Copper Company in New York City purchased four streetcars to transport miners in Helena. Before going into service, however, those streetcars were put into service in Butte, Montana.

Building in quality was the overriding concern of Mr. P.A. who personally supervised the 10 engineering employees.

Thomas could not abide a poor mechanic or a woodworking employee who did not fulfill the expectations the man had raised in his interview. Perley A. Thomas Car Works paid up to 80 cents an hour, far more than what most of the companies in High Point were paying. Mr. P.A. expected to get good workers for such good money.

He once recruited at least 20 supposedly experienced employees from a streetcar manufacturer in St. Louis. Within months, more than half of the men had returned to the Midwest. They were either unable or unwilling to comply with Mr. P.A.'s expectations in woodwork and engineering skills.

Those who could meet his demands had long careers with the company. Chris Schultheiss started as an engineer and draftsman manufacturing streetcars. His son Clarence would

The National Brake Company, Inc. Of Buffalo, N.Y. thought enough of Perley A. Thomas to use its streetcars in its brake advertising. The streetcar shown here was sold and used in San Juan, Puerto Rico. These were single-end cars, meaning controls were only at one end and the streetcar systems had turnarounds at the end of the track.

be plant superintendent for many years. Men like Archie Allred, Harry Halker, Jerome Hutchens, Jim Wrenn, Art and Clayner Shipwash all heard about the high quality Mr. P.A. demanded and they joined the company to help produce it.

Although he was a demanding employer, Thomas was also a forgiving man. Family members recall many times when employees would quit when Mr. P.A. would pointedly, sometimes loudly, question the quality of their work. Thomas would visit the men that night, apologize for his outburst, then ask them to return to work. They usually did because they had confidence in their temperamental boss. They knew his demands for quality would insure them of a job if his concern translated to new and repeat business.

The business did come, but not without production headaches. These problems were most often caused by the transit companies. Every city's transit company demanded that manufacturers design streetcars that fit their own set of individualized specifications. This meant that no streetcar manufacturer could truly standardize design. Even if a company had a catalog of existing designs it had already produced, each city transit company would demand its own distinctive streetcar models.

Sometimes a city's streetcars varied from one year to the next, simply because the person in charge of writing specifications had been replaced. At one point, Perley A. Thomas Car Works had a catalog that showed 41 different streetcar designs. Some designs were already operating and some were proposed streetcars Thomas had included in a marketing effort to get cities to standardize their orders. He never succeeded. Neither did any other streetcar manufacturer.

Each city had variations in body length, passenger capacity, door width, control placement, and the positioning of the fare box. The fare box location depended on whether the car had a two-man crew of motorman and conductor, or just a motorman. Some cities demanded narrow doors at the front of the cars and wide doors in the center. Other cities would demand wide doors in the front and narrow doors

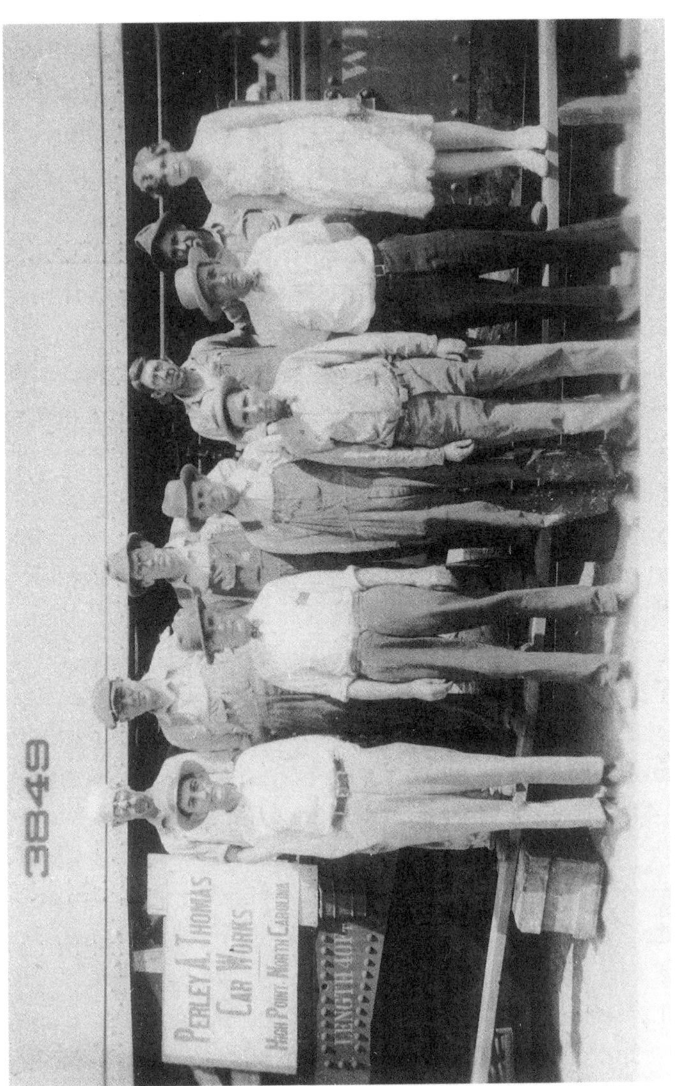

Perley A. Thomas Car Works supervisors and the company secretary pose before one of "The Detroiters" loaded on a railway flatcar on its way to Michigan. The Detroiters were made in 1930 and were the last major order the company filled. Left to right bottom row—Art Shipwash, Chris Schultheis, Mr. Burton, Clayner Shipwash, Archie Allred and Etta York. Top Row-Walt Henderson, Harry Halker, Jerome Hutchens, Carl Wright, J.H. Everhart.

Of proven value in any community

Some communities served by "Thomas-Built" Cars

Augusta, Ga.
Helena, Mont.
Miami, Fla.
Durham, N. C.
Trenton, N. J.
New Orleans, La.
Hampton, Va.
Sheffield, Ala.
Danville, Va.
Greenville, S. C.

Augusta, Ga.

Sheffield, Ala.

Miami, Fla.

New Orleans, La.

"Thomas-Built" Cars

If you judge cars on the basis of lower operating costs and increased passenger revenue, "Thomas-Built" Cars have certainly proved their worth.

At the same time their extreme safety, attractive appearance and unusual comfort make them a welcome asset in any community.

Note the list of prominent installations on the other page—typical of many more cities being served by "Thomas-Built" Cars.

Let us demonstrate with figures what "Thomas-Built" Cars have accomplished on well-known electric railways—and what you may expect them to accomplish for you.

PERLEY A. THOMAS CAR WORKS
High Point, N.C.

Perley A. Thomas Car Works usually used its products as its best advertising as seen in this two-page advertisement showing four different cars used in four different cities.

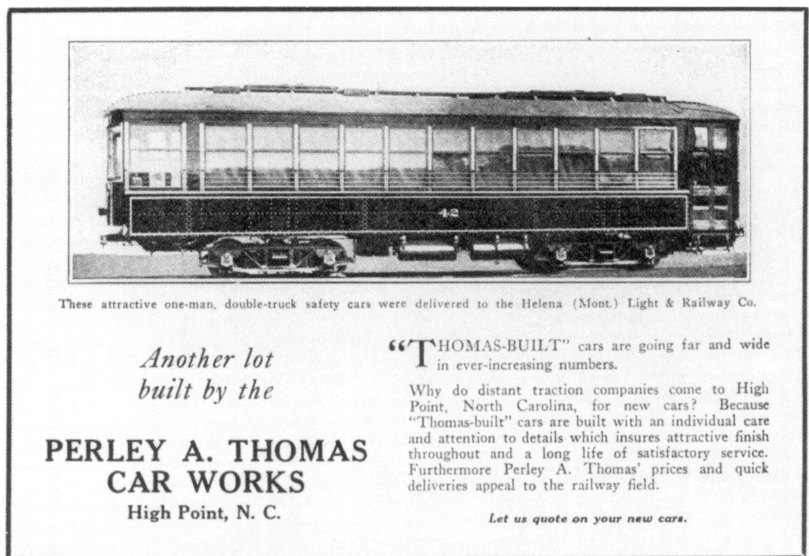

This ad shows the Helena, Mont. streetcar and asks the question; "Why do distant traction companies come to High Point?" Naturally, it was because that is where the "Thomas Built" cars were made.

in the center. In the days of two crewmen, some cities would put fare boxes at the front and middle, allowing passengers two entry points. When the conductor's position was eliminated, all passengers were required to board at the front of the car where the motorman could monitor the fare box.

The number of doors was usually governed by the presence of a loop track at the end of the line. If there was a loop track, doors might only be installed on the right side of the car. If there was no loop track, doors would be installed on both sides so passengers could always board from the sidewalk no matter which direction the car was headed.

The seats, frequently made out of rattan, were ingeniously designed with reversible backs. When the streetcar reached the end of the line, the conductor would walk down the rows and

Not all cars were large. This Birney Car No. 106 made for Mobile, Ala. featured single-trucks. (William D. Middleton collection)

pull the seat backs toward him so riders getting on for the return trip would be facing forward.

One of Mr. P.A.'s business strengths was the ability to listen to the needs of the transit companies then transform those specifications quickly into blueprints. According to his family, Thomas' mind started thinking of design as the transit company buyer began talking. Frequently, he could sketch out what the buyer wanted before leaving the man's office. If there was agreement, it was a matter of returning to High Point to draw the precise blueprints, then build the streetcars to the agreed-upon specifications.

Mr. P.A.'s ability to sketch out a design while talking with a potential customer made him an excellent salesman. In fact, he personally performed all of the company's selling and negotiation of the bids with the exception of the last two orders for Mobile and Knoxville. Those two orders were sold by his son, Norman.

Mr. P.A. fit in socially whether the city was New York, Knoxville or Winston-Salem. He always donned three piece suits, even when coming to work in the factory in High Point.

He sometimes wore fancy spats (buttoned, cloth coverings that fit over the tops of shoes and socks between the instep and ankle). Early in his career he wore a handlebar mustache. An accomplished musician who would play the guitar and the harmonica at the same time to amuse his grandsons, he loved taking his wife Margaret dancing. He was the perfect image of a successful 1920's businessman.

At the same time, he could fit right in with the men on the factory floor. Although a trolley stop was close to his house, he would frequently walk the two miles to his factory. As was the custom of the times, he chewed and smoked cigars. He had an unerring aim when he had to spit out the tobacco residue. According to his sons, there were several holes drilled in the elevated floor of the engineering office which allowed air to circulate up through the room. Mr. P.A. would be drawing blueprints of streetcars when he would turn, aim, and hit a selected hole with a bit of chewed cigar, all without lifting his pencil from the paper.

By 1924, Perley A. Thomas Car Works was running ads proclaiming: "Thomas Built cars are going everywhere in ever-increasing numbers. Why do traction companies come to High Point, North Carolina, for new cars? Because 'Thomas Built cars' are built with an individual care and attention to details that insures attractive finish throughout and a long life of satisfactory service. Furthermore, Perley A. Thomas' prices and quick deliveries appeal to the railway field. Let us quote on your new cars."

Another Thomas ad from 1925 shows one of six cars built for the Southern Public Utilities Company of Greenville, South Carolina: "More Thomas Cars For the South. Thomas Cars are built to conform with the best railway practice. Our best testimonials are repeat orders. Let us quote on your requirements."

Most manufacturers did not scrimp on the interior appointments of their cars. One description of Southern Car Company cars (which matches the description of an early New Orleans order) describes "Enameled stanchions placed as to encourage passengers to take the proper handhold in boarding and alighting...instead of hand straps, white enameled tubing is arranged over the longitudinal seats in a horizontal position convenient for handholds...the floor is of tongue and groove yellow pine with the roof of half inch poplar with number eight canvas duck...The interior finish is dark cherry color with light green trim and the outside of the car is painted dark green."

In 1924 Perley A. Thomas Car Works was at the peak of its business. Inside the factory were three pairs of rails constituting the assembly line. That allowed room for up to nine cars to be under construction at once by the 125-man work force. Teams of workers would build the streetcars with each trolley moving twice during its assembly. It took about six days to build each streetcar with the factory turning out an average of seven per week. Each streetcar was hand sanded inside and out. All painting was brush work.

The company had already delivered 25 streetcars to New Orleans and had just received an order for 55 more when disaster struck. A fire, apparently starting in a clogged-up dust removal system, swept through the plant, destroying 14 of the New Orleans streetcars in various stages of completion. No one was hurt since the fire started at night after the shift was over, but the plant was severely damaged.

Within a few hours of the fire, the president of the J.G. Brill Car Company in Philadelphia called Thomas with an offer. If Thomas would agree not to reopen the factory, Brill would pay him a five-year contract at $5,000 per year, or it would pay him $25,000 in cash immediately.

Thomas refused. Instead, he took a $100,000 advance order check from New Orleans for the undelivered 55 cars, and immediately bought the electric motors he would need to fill the New Orleans order. History does not record if any New Orleans transit officials ever learned of the fire, but they did not cancel their order. Had they backed out, that would have been the death knell of the company. Thomas filled that 55-car order, plus another 25-car order. Over 12 years, New Orleans bought more than 100 streetcars from Perley A. Thomas Car Works, almost one fourth of the company's total production in 13 years. Today, all of the streetcars running in New Orleans are Perley A. Thomas models manufactured after the fire.

By the late 1920's, streetcar orders were beginning to slow. For instance, the Alabama Power Company bought a single Thomas streetcar in 1926 for use in Sheffield. Mr. P.A. did not pass up the opportunity to advertise even this small sale. A catalog description of "The Sheffield" claims "Performance records kept on the Sheffield model have proven the economy of operating this style car. At the same time the records show patronage has increased, which means the car has paid its own way. Here is the answer to your transportation problems. The Sheffield type may not fill the needs of your particular city, but we can build one that will. Thomas Built cars are serving many communities and can serve yours as well."

The ad did not yield many new customers. Macon, Georgia, bought 12 streetcars from Perley A. Thomas Car Works in 1927. Greenville, North Carolina, bought five in 1929.

The Knoxville Power & Light Company purchased ten 44-passenger cars in late 1929 at a cost of $14,000 per unit, $10 under the offer of the next closest bidder. Thomas then tried to drum up more business with a catalog description that played on Knoxville's confidence in Perley A. Thomas Car Works: "An order for ten of these new light weight, all steel cars of the

In 1928

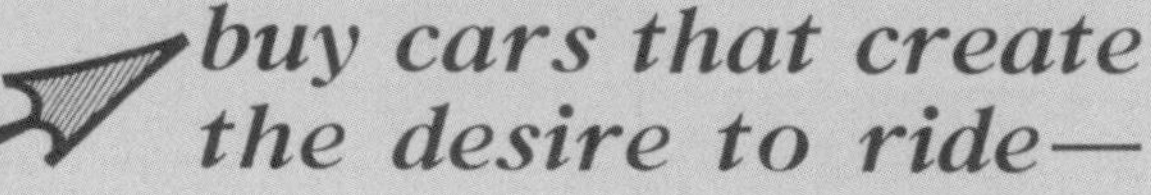

and to repeat a comfortable ride—

buy

"Thomas-Built"
Cars

Some
communities
served by
"Thomas-Built"
Cars

Augusta, Ga.
Helena, Mont.
Miami, Fla.
Durham, N. C.
Trenton, N. J.
New Orleans, La.
Hampton, Va.
Sheffield, Ala.
Danville, Va.
Greenville, S. C.

Their extreme safety, attractive appearance and unusual comfort make them a welcome asset in any community.

And on the basis of lower operating costs and maintenance expense, "*Thomas-Built*" Cars have certainly proved their worth.

Note the list of prominent installations—typical of the many other cities being served by "*Thomas-Built*" Cars.

What you may expect "*Thomas-Built*" Cars to accomplish for you, might be demonstrated with figures of what they have accomplished on other well-known electric railways. Shall we send you these figures?

PERLEY A. THOMAS CAR WORKS
High Point, N. C.

By 1928, Perley A. Thomas seemed to sense market problems. This ad urged transit companies to buy cars that would "create the desire to ride."

one man, double end, double truck, and arch roof type has just been completed and delivered to the Knoxville, Tennessee Power & Light Company. Sufficient strength to meet all requirements, yet sufficiently light to permit economical operation, these cars have won the praises of operators and patrons alike."

THOMAS BUILT CARS
For Knoxville Power & Light Company
Knoxville, Tenn.

TO ASSURE their passengers the utmost in comfort, efficiency and safety, the progressive management of the Knoxville Power & Light Company recently placed 10 "Thomas-built cars" in service. Almost over night the new cars won the praises of both passengers and operator alike.

These attractive new lightweight all-steel cars of the one-man, double-end, double-truck and arch-roof type are designed for economical and satisfactory service with sufficient strength to meet all requirements and yet not be of excessive weight.

A shrinking market may be reflected in the fact that the company was now emphasizing purchases by individual customers.

The largest single Perley A. Thomas Car Works' streetcar order in its history was one of its last. In late 1929 The City of Detroit ordered 100 "two-man, single-end (meaning drive controls were at one end), center-exit, double-truck type cars" as they were described in a catalog. The cars were the longest the company had ever made, more than 48 feet long. They also had the largest capacity, 52 passengers. The width of the front door was also the largest the company had ever produced; five feet, four inches.

The Detroiter pictured above was part of an order for 100 streetcars placed on November 19, 1928. Delivery was completed only six months later on May 17, 1929.

The Thomas catalog on this streetcar seemed to predict the coming demise of the streetcar industry. In describing "The Detroiter" the brochure explains: "Because the problem of transportation is today a selling job as in everything else, no street railway car can be too comfortable, too attractive or too safe. Realizing this, we have spared no effort to make the occasional rider become a regular patron by making him as comfortable as possible and his surroundings as pleasant as possible. A year of service with these cars has borne out our contention that patrons and owners are both well pleased."

Greensboro, just 20 miles from High Point, bought some Perley A. Thomas cars in the late 1920's.

They may have been "well-pleased," but that did not stop the City of Detroit from scrapping the streetcars less than 25 years after purchasing them. By 1953 the last of the most modern of the Perley A. Thomas Car Works streetcars were junked.

The last order for four streetcars came from Mobile, Alabama, in 1930. It had been a marvelous, if short, run of business. In 15 years, the Perley A. Thomas Car Works had built more than 400 streetcars.

CHAPTER 4

Streetcars Die; Buses Are Born

Many factors contributed to the death of the streetcar manufacturing business. (While the streetcar manufacturing business was dying, some cities continued to operate them well into the 1950's and 1960's. New Orleans is the only United States city that never completely killed streetcar service and other cities may bring them back. Toronto, Ontario, reintroduced modern streetcars to its streets several years ago. Their streetcars look much like 1920's models.)

Perhaps the most important factor contributing to the demise of streetcars was The Great Depression. Electric power companies and municipalities, the two leading purchasers of trolleys, fared little better than the average citizen when it came to having money during the late 1920's and 1930's. The private power companies, which had pioneered mass transit in most cities, were getting out of the business because they wanted to concentrate on wiring the country. They asked the cities to take over streetcar systems where often controlled fares had increased little in more than 10 years.

Even when there was money in the cities' coffers, there was pressure from companies like General Motors to switch

This is downtown Knoxville, TN, probably in 1930. This Thomas streetcar was later sold to a streetcar line in Waterloo, Iowa. It is still running today. (Joe Bell collection.)

from electric streetcars to gasoline or diesel powered buses. GM made a strong case for buses over trolleys by pointing out buses could turn down any street in the city while trolleys were restricted to those streets where tracks had been laid. Many cities agreed and often even gave up their claims to right-of-ways. Rails were dug up or buried under asphalt.

For a while, companies like Perley A. Thomas Car Works made an effort to fight back, or at least compromise with the cities on a vision for mass transit. Thomas built two "trolley coaches" for the City of Greensboro, North Carolina, and another two for the City of Greenville, South Carolina in 1934. The trolley coach was a hybrid of the streetcar and the bus; an electric-powered, rubber-tired bus that could move to the curb to pick up passengers, then swing back into the center of the street underneath the electric power lines.

Thomas was uncomfortable with the concept of the trolley coach from the beginning. While the vehicle was not restricted by rails, it required a dedicated electric line so there was still no answer to GM's claim that buses could go down any street. On top of that, citizens were complaining more often about an unfortunate side effect of electric powered vehicles passing their homes. (The passing of the trolley coach would cause interference with home A.M. radio reception.)

The Perley A. Thomas Car Works electric trolley coach did not satisfy its manufacturer or its potential customers. Only four were made.

Sometime during the manufacture of Greensboro's trolley coaches in 1934, Perley A. Thomas Car Works also got a small order for ten transit buses from Duke Power in Anderson, South Carolina.

The order was quickly filled. It made little money because it had been a small order, not enough to build hopes that there was a future in manufacturing transit buses. Still, there was something about that small order that made the company's

The first buses manufactured by Perley A. Thomas Car Works were for the municipal transit company in Anderson, South Carolina. They were built in 1934, two years before the company-saving order for school buses came from the North Carolina school system.

workers and the owners feel very good about their ability to deliver a quality product.

For the second time in 15 years, Perley A. Thomas was facing a personal financial crisis. The first time, he had been an employee of a failed company. That had not been so bad. He had his woodworking tools. He had his sense of design. He knew he could make a living making mantels, chairs, tables and church altars.

This time was different. He was the owner of a company that teetered on the brink of failure. He had family money invested in the venture. There was a daughter at home to support and two sons who worked for him. He had employees, some of whom he had recruited from hundreds of miles away based on his promise that they would find work with him.

As Thomas struggled to keep his factory open, he reluctantly cut his work force. A factory that once had 125 men racing each other to sand and paint streetcars seemed cavernous when the work force dwindled to under a dozen. There just was nothing to be built that needed Thomas' factory. By the early 1930's the company was in receivership and Thomas was back to hand crafting furniture when he could find customers. He put all of his earnings back into the company. Willard was forced to drop out of Elon College after just one semester.

Thomas did not hire many new employees during this darkest time in the company's history, but he did hire one in 1929 who proved to be a strong asset in future years. That was his oldest child, Melva. She had gone to school longer than anyone else in the family, through the tenth grade. After she graduated from a business school where she studied bookkeeping, she moved to Ft. Macon, Georgia, during World War I. It was there that she met William Hughes Price. After marrying, the two returned to High Point, where she took a job as bookkeeper for a local car dealer.

Hired as bookkeeper by her father, Melva Thomas Price also served as payroll supervisor, secretary to the president, office and insurance manager and check writer. Monitoring the company's money was a job she took to heart. She knew when a customer's check had cleared the bank and how long to wait before anyone at Perley A. Thomas Car Works could write a check on those funds. When company employees, including her brothers, went to Melva with a check request, she wanted to know why that purchase was necessary. Even the request to purchase a bag of nails from the local hardware store received careful consideration from Melva and Willard.

The brothers usually trusted their sister when it came to the question of money. In the 1950's when the company was on more solid financial ground, Norman sent his sons Jim and Albert to Buffalo, New York, to buy three 300-ton steel presses. Jim called his aunt Melva to report that all three presses were in good shape and right for purchase. Melva told him he could buy only one. Jim told his aunt that his father had authorized them to buy all three. Melva listened politely then wired enough money to buy one press. Jim and Albert came home with just one press. According to the family, Melva won most arguments with her father and brothers when it came to spending money.

But that family story would have never happened had the company not survived some hard times in the mid-1930's. The problem was simple to understand. After the Mobile streetcar order, the Perley A. Thomas Car Works was without a product, direction, or a future.

Then in 1936 the state of North Carolina put out a request for bids to build 500 school buses that would be scattered throughout the 100 North Carolina counties. That sounded promising. After all, the family reasoned, it had built the Anderson, South Carolina transit buses just two years earlier. True, it had been a small job, but the company could legitimately claim to have manufactured buses. The family believed its lasting national reputation as a manufacturer of streetcars should carry some weight with the state's officials.

There was one slight problem in answering the bid. The company's finances had grown so tight that it lacked the petty cash to even send Norman and Willard to Raleigh to see the bus on which the company was to bid. They borrowed a car and cash from their mother's personal savings account to buy gasoline for the trip.

The Thomas brothers were shocked when they pulled into the state garage lot to inspect the school bus that could mean the difference between closing their factory, or perhaps launching them on a new career path. They were literally speechless as the state officials pointed out the physical characteristics of the school bus they wanted some company to build.

The Perley A. Thomas Car Works had built its reputation by providing customers with the finest in workmanship and incorporating the latest in design techniques. Mr. P.A. would spend days hunched over his drawing board creating designs that would make the streetcars that bore his name better, stronger and safer. He had always insisted that the best materials go into the company's trolleys. He bought only the best rolled steel to form the streetcars. The driving gears and electric motors were bought from the top suppliers.

The school bus the Thomas factory would have to copy was nothing like the quality-built, high technology transportation that had carried the family name from New York to New Orleans. North Carolina education officials were taking bids to manufacture 500 school buses using outdated designs and techniques.

More than 10 years after streetcar manufacturers had shifted to all-steel construction, North Carolina's school bus bodies were still made of wood. Well, it was almost all wood. The roof was made of tin, which did little more than keep the rain out. The seats were wooden benches that ran longitudinal to the frame of the bus instead of the forward-facing seats that were common on streetcars and virtually every other public conveyance in the state. The bus had one windshield wiper on the left side on the presumption that the driver need only look straight ahead and not out the right half of the windshield. The vehicle had no mirrors, based on the assumption that the driver would always be looking straight ahead. Perhaps the most amazing thing the brothers encountered was that the bus had no headlights. Even streetcars had headlights!

Although all automobiles and trucks had been equipped for decades with headlights installed at the factory, the school bus specifications forbade them. The headlights were rejected by the state's bid writers on the apparent grounds that school buses ran only in daylight hours, thus headlights would serve no purpose. The brothers would have to figure in the cost of removing the headlights from the bus chassis in its bid to the state of North Carolina.

Norman and Willard went to Raleigh determined not to leave until they knew every inch of the sample bus they intended to manufacture in their now idle High Point factory. Nothing was overlooked. Although they were only bidding on the job of adding a bus body to a delivered chassis, they learned all they could about the other components of the bus. They measured the frame down to a sixteenth of an inch. They measured the thickness of the wood posts holding the body to the frame. They even counted the exact number of bolts holding the school bus body onto the frame. They knew that bus before they left Raleigh.

Norman, Willard and Melva huddled with their father to prepare their bid. They priced every component of the bus body starting with a price assigned to the lowliest bolt and nut. They shaved every expense to the bone, knowing that they had to beat a number of other, more experienced North Carolina bus manufacturers. The competition was not kind to the newcomers. They spread rumors about Perley A. Thomas Car Work's inability to meet both the bid's financing and its specifications. One of the competitor-launched rumors that reached the education department was that the company did not have the thick oak supports necessary to secure the bus body to the frame.

These brand new buses belong to the Avery County, N.C. schools. The photo is from 1937, the year after Thomas first started building buses. The cars probably belong to employees.

Mr. P.A. fired off a letter to the state board of education confirming that the company did indeed have the wooden supports. He invited state officials to visit the factory to prove that the supports were in stock. N.C. School Transportation Superintendent C.C. Brown liked the style of this little High Point company.

Perley A. Thomas Car Works did indeed have the oak supports of the thickness specified in the bid. In fact, that is about the only thing in the factory that even resembled the components of a school bus. Those wooden supports happened to be the same size that had been commonly used in the manufacture of wooden streetcars when the company started its manufacturing line in 1917. When Perley A. Thomas Car Works switched to making steel streetcars, the extra wooden supports had been relegated to a work shed. Mr. P.A. had been sure he could find a use for them some day. If nothing else, they could have been used as firewood.

The successful transition of Perley A. Thomas Car Works from a North Carolina-based streetcar manufacturer to the largest school bus manufacturer in the world can be traced directly to the fact that the founder of the company loved a well-turned piece of wood. The company's possession of those antiquated wooden supports proved to the state of North Carolina that Perley A. Thomas Car Works was a legitimate manufacturer of school buses.

Mary Thomas

Melva Thomas

Norman Thomas

Willard Thomas

Chapter 5

Willard, Norman and Melva Get Their Chance

The school bus bids Perley A. Thomas Car Works submitted to the state of North Carolina sound small today, even when compared to the $7,000 cost of a 52-passenger all-steel streetcar in 1929. Thomas told the state that it based its bid on building 200 of the original 500 bus order since it could afford to finance only 200. The company's bid was $195 to build a 17-foot long bus; $205 to build a 19-footer and $225 for a 21-foot school bus. The state awarded Thomas the contract with little fanfare and the future of Perley A. Thomas Car Works was settled. At least it appeared so in 1936.

When word reached the unemployed and underemployed citizens of High Point that the company had guaranteed money under a state contract, a rush for jobs resulted. More than 100 job applicants lined up at the factory before daylight the day after the contract was awarded. The family never found out how the word of the job openings had leaked. They never even advertised or officially put out a call for new employees. The workers came to them, eager to start at 35 cents an hour. In the 1920's near the end of the streetcar manufacturing days, the company had paid up to 85 cents an hour and was one of the highest paying companies in Guilford County. In Depression-era North Carolina, 35 cents an hour was a Godsend.

The original order for the school buses was completed in five months. When the last school bus rolled out the door of the factory, Melva announced that the company checking account had more money in it than it did before the school bus order. The company, once close to folding, had made a profit.

That first bus order, while establishing Perley A. Thomas Car Works as a transportation manufacturer again, did not instantly put the company on firm financial ground. The order had been for only 200 buses. Once those were completed, other work had to be found. As the Depression began to ease in the late 1930's, the company manufactured some travel trailers. These 15-foot, 19-foot and 21-foot trailers were towed behind cars.

Just as he had with his streetcars, Thomas insisted that his woodworkers put extra touches into the trailers so they would stand out from cheaper competition. Perley A. Thomas Car Works' travel trailers even had a bathroom—a wooden box with a toilet seat mounted on top. Inside the box was a five-gallon bucket. For years after those Thomas trailers went on—and off—the market, satisfied customers from around the country would drive all the way to High Point trying to buy Thomas trailers. They were particularly popular with traveling carnivals. The family remembers an old carnival woman who came to High Point virtually insisting that Perley A. Thomas Car Works start production of the trailers once again. She threatened to hex them if they did not restart the manufacturing line. The family refused to make any more trailers and no calamity befell the company.

The company looked into making anything on wheels. It successfully bid on a fleet of bakery trucks. A dairy had the

The interior of a Perley A. Thomas Car Works trailer. These were particularly popular with traveling carnival workers.

company build bodies on its trucks so it could transport milk. Both were questionable ventures that made the family uneasy since they knew little about those industries. What appealed to Norman, Willard and Melva, now in their mid-30's, was the transportation industry. They knew how to move people from one place to another. They decided that bus builders they were, and bus builders they would be.

By the late 1930's, Mr. P.A. was ready to let his children start taking the company wherever they wanted it to go. He was in his mid-50's and had begun to tire of the daily grind of running a growing company. Being a company president meant reading profit and loss statements, projecting income and expenses, looking for new customers and keeping old customers. That was not what he wanted to do.

Perley A. Thomas was what 1990's management consultants would call a "classic" entrepreneur. He was a designer of things. It did not matter if it was a chair, a streetcar or a school bus body. If the project allowed him to sit at a drafting table and put his visions on paper, he liked it. Once he had the design on paper, he liked to figure out how to build it. That was how he wanted to spend his working days.

Starting the streetcar company was almost incidental to the thrill he got from designing the streetcars. He did not like the tedium of coming to work every day to focus on the things that make a corporation grow. He was a designer at heart, not a corporation president. He sought the thrill of developing something new.

In 1938, before the federal government mandated safety requirements, most bus manufacturers created a bus body frame by bolting or welding three pieces of steel together to form a bow. That was then welded to the top edge of the bus floor. Mr. P.A. looked at that three-piece bow design and decided that it did not give the same safety that a single piece bent into a true bow shape would have. His design had no overhead bolts or welds that could fail in case of crash or rollover. He also decided to extend the bow to the outside of the frame and weld it outside. That put the ribs of the bow below the floor by several inches and created a structural member that provided real security to the passengers. Mr. P.A. reasoned that this design, which put vertical steel members some inches lower than his competitors, would help keep smaller vehicles from running underneath the bus thus reduce the danger of the bus overturning.

More than 40 years after Mr. P.A. had perfected his extended bow concept, Thomas Built Buses had a structural engineering professor at North Carolina State University examine his design. The professor with the advanced degree

The interior of an early Thomas bus. Note the bench setting running the length of the bus rather than individual seats.

could not find any needed improvements to the design created by the self-taught structural engineer. Mr. P.A. was right, as usual. The company still employs the basic design.

Mr. P.A., following through on a promise he made to his children, began to turn over control of the company to them. In return, the children gave him an employment contract, a monthly salary and a promise that he would receive the same percentage raise that the family members gave themselves.

That contract was not a way for his children to ease their father out of the company he had founded. They needed his design expertise. He had always been and continued to be the company's best designer and mechanical problem solver. On several occasions after he had "retired" and moved to Florida, he was brought back to work on critical projects.

Mr. P.A.'s children inherited his commitment to hard work. They developed their own standards for helping the company grow much larger than he had ever dreamed. Starting in the late 1930's and continuing through the 1940's, the siblings fully dedicated themselves to making the company grow. They

Mr. P.A. Thomas with his four children circa 1950. From left to right—younger son, Norman; younger daughter, Mary; Mr. P.A.; older daughter, Melva; and older son, Willard.

put in eight hours at the plant, went home for supper, then returned to work until 11:00 p.m. Saturday was just another work day. Their spouses were working just as hard. Norman's wife, Mary, was a nurse. Willard's wife, Mavis, was a school teacher. Melva's husband, Bill, worked for the Southern Railway.

There was no such thing as "child day care" in those days. When they could not stay at home, the third generation children, Pat (using his initials of Perley A. II), Jim, John, Albert and Bill would play outside the plant. When they got tired, they would curl up in the back seats of the cars as they waited for their parents.

There was never any question among the siblings about who would run the company. All of them would share in the responsibilities.

Long before women held management roles in most companies, Melva and Mary were treated as equals by their brothers. When the siblings went into a room to make a major decision, everyone had an equal say. The four of them would sit around and thrash out whatever problem the company was facing at the time.

And, according to family, these were not always friendly discussions. Though personally close, the Thomas children were all business at work. Their personalities and business styles sometimes clashed. When one would offer a proposal on an action the company should take, the others would sometimes challenge the idea. The person offering the plan could expect his or her siblings to demand details before they were satisfied. The family personalities assured that intense discussion would take place. It did.

Willard, who acted as company president for over 20 years, was conservative and a careful planner. He wanted to study proposals before acting on them. No detail was too small. For instance, he routinely checked his night watchmen's punch clock tape to make sure they made their rounds. At the same time, Willard dealt with larger issues like working with the bankers and attorneys. He monitored the cost of production and was the first in the family to realize they had to find sales outside North Carolina to secure the long term future of the company. Willard travelled extensively throughout the Southeast in the early 1940's calling on school boards to sell buses, while at the same time, looking for potential sales representatives. This was the beginning of a national distribution system.

For all his conservatism, Willard also took an interest in the creative side of the business, coordinating the production of advertising and sales literature. Family members say he enjoyed helping write the advertisements and directing photographers.

Norman was more like his father. He was quicker to make decisions and conscious of slowness in his employees. If his engineers were behind in delivering a project, he wanted to know why and how long it would be before they finished. Norman liked working with engineering, production, purchasing and labor relations. Forced by federal government law to accept a labor union in the company's factory during World War II, Norman made regaining direct control of his employees one of his goals. It took some time, but the union eventually left the company.

Melva was the tough compromiser. She would listen to Willard's suggestions to go slower and to Norman's suggestions to go faster. She would then help mediate an agreement that everyone could accept. She went into every meeting knowing how much money was in the company's accounts.

Mary, the youngest sister by 14 years, was the careful listener. She would usually cast her vote after most of the arguments had been settled.

While the Thomas children always said they did not inherit their father's design skills, they did have the family ability to put aside business disagreements. Just as Mr. P.A. could scold employees in the morning and apologize to them in the evening, his children could loudly argue the future of the company in a staff meeting then work side by side moments later. The siblings never took personal offense when their business ideas were under scrutiny.

Mr. P.A.'s children never ever let their positions in the company go to their heads. Job titles were not important to them. Even after their years of hard work had put the company on solid financial ground, the idea of cashing in or creating perks for themselves never occurred to Willard, Norman, Melva and Mary. For example, there was only one company car when the second generation ran Perley A. Thomas Car Works and it was for running errands. There were no fancy offices or even telephones on every desk. When Willard and Norman grew tired of walking into Melva's office to answer a telephone call, they saw no need to install an extension in their office. They simply knocked a hole in the wall so Melva could pass the telephone through to them.

Executive titles meant little. The titles of president, vice president and secretary/treasurer were formalities on which the government insisted. It became a family joke: "Well, who do you want to be today—president or vice president?" The Thomas family was comfortable knowing that when they went into a room, they all had equal voices. When they emerged, all would abide by the decisions reached. Most family meetings were short. There were buses to be built and meetings took away from work time.

While Willard and Norman likely never knew it, their sons growing up around the company could always tell when their fathers were agreeing on a design change. When Willard and Norman would be standing at the drafting table, they would lean forward. As the discussion for the design change would near agreement, both men, anxious to end the conversation and move on to something else, would begin tapping their toes. Their sons started kidding them about tap dancing.

Though times sometimes seemed tough during the 1930's and 1940's as Mr. P.A. phased himself out of actively running the company, orders were increasing. In 1938 Mr. P.A. designed the state's first all-steel school bus body and North Carolina ordered 400 buses. In 1940 it ordered 900 more. The state now knew the company and trusted it. Within a few years, the fear that the company could fail again had passed.

Part of the reason for success was that Perley A. Thomas Car Works had perfected school bus improvements that proved both rational and popular with school administrators. While the company was still restricted by state specifications, Thomas designers worked to develop safety advantages. One was a front engine cowl made of much heavier steel to provide greater resistance in head-on collisions.

Another improvement was the development of outward-opening doors. Before the Thomas design, most competitors folded their doors; one door would open in while the other would open out. Mr. P.A. reasoned that in an accident the mechanism for folding the doors could be damaged, which would prevent the doors from folding in properly. His design was for bus doors to open outward. Even if the doors were damaged in a crash, the driver or the children could still force them open.

The bus manufacturing business was going well in 1941 when Perley A. Thomas Car Works faced its third financial challenge. First the streetcar factory had burned down in 1924. Then the streetcar business had folded in 1930 with the coming of diesel buses, the automobile and The Great Depression.

Now a second world war was threatening to stop the company from building its principal products. One of the last prewar orders for buses that the company received was from the U.S. Marine Corps. The buses would be used to transport new recruits at Camp Lejune, North Carolina. Once the United States entered the war, school bus manufacturing virtually ceased. The federal government was more concerned about conserving resources for the national war effort than it was in making buses for state school systems.

The only solution Willard and Norman could think of to keep the company going was to build something for the war effort. Again, they called on their father to help them. What Mr. P.A. designed may have saved thousands of American lives during World War II.

Soon after the war started and bus production was halted, Willard, Norman and Mr. P.A. boarded a train to an Army camp in New Jersey. It was there that a U.S. Army colonel agreed to meet with them concerning his idea for a mobile small arms repair facility that could be mounted on the back of an Army truck.

A mobile small arms repair shop manufactured by Perley A. Thomas Car Works during World War II.

The colonel had recognized an inherent problem in the nation's drive to produce weapons. The country's major industrial plants were running 24 hours a day turning out rifles, machine guns and pistols. Ignored to that point was how to repair those small arms in the field. The Army could put millions of new weapons onto the battlefield, but when those guns malfunctioned, there was no clean facility available for their repair.

As Mr. P.A. listened to the colonel talk, he examined and measured an Army truck. He then sketched a design for a six-foot by six-foot metal shell with windows and work benches built into the shell. He handed the paper to the colonel and asked if that design was what the officer had in mind. Before they left the base or even worked up the cost of what the Army called "a mobile repair shop," they had an order in hand for the Perley A. Thomas Car Works.

When the brothers and Mr. P.A. returned to High Point, they noticed two of their competitors climbing off another railroad car on the same train. The men, who competed with Thomas on bus contracts, wanted to know if Mr. P.A. had been successful in finding business with the government.

While they did not accuse them to their faces, the Thomas family knew that their competitors had engaged in some low level, if clumsy, industrial espionage. Somehow the men had learned of Mr. P.A.'s contact with the Army and had followed the family all the way to New Jersey and back.

While Mr. P.A. may have been able to secure an exclusive contract for his company with the Army, he did not try. Instead, he freely shared his mobile repair shop plans with his competitors. There is no Thomas record that he ever charged his competitors anything for access to his plans. It was his way of contributing to the war effort.

No one with the company remembers how many mobile arms repair shops were manufactured, but the company produced 15 per day, every day. Thousands of mobile repair shops built by Perley A. Thomas Car Works were sent to all theaters of operations. The U.S. Signal Corps contacted the company with its own specifications for a mobile signaling facility. Thomas also made metal pontoons for use by Army engineers to bridge rivers.

With the Army, however, came something that Perley A. Thomas Car Works had never had. That was a labor union. To make sure that labor strife did not disrupt the round-the-clock manufacturing going on all over the nation, the federal government required that all its manufacturers of transportation equipment invite the United Auto Workers to organize their work forces. The union remained for nearly 20 years before being voted out by employees who trusted that the third generation of the Thomas family would provide them the good working conditions and fringe benefits the union could only promise.

When World War II ended, millions of soldiers, sailors and airmen came home to get married and raise families. The children of all those postwar families would soon need something the Thomas family knew how to provide—school buses.

"The Boys" pose in The Charlotte Trolley (a hand-built streetcar that closely resembles a Thomas streetcar) Left to Right: Jim Thomas, Albert Thomas, Bill Price, John W. Thomas, Jr. and Pat Thomas. (John Russell photo)

CHAPTER 6

Here Come the Boys!

During and immediately after World War II, the last of Mr. P.A.'s children and the first of his grandchildren started working for the company.

Mary, the only child of Mr. P.A. and Margaret born in High Point, was almost 14 years younger than Norman, the next youngest. She watched her father, sister and two brothers work in the family business for years as she went to high school and business school. Somehow she resisted the lure of making it a complete family business until 1946, when at the age of 29, she finally agreed to become Norman's secretary. Skilled at taking short hand, she soon was taking and placing orders over the telephone. Mary worked for the company from 1946 to 1982, retiring as assistant secretary to the corporation. She died in 1983.

Mary's niece, although almost her same age, was Dorothy "Dot" Price Webb, the daughter of William and Melva Thomas Price. Dot started working for Perley A. Thomas Car Works in 1942 and retired in 1971 as assistant treasurer of the company. Her reputation was much softer than her mother's, but she never let that stand in the way of negotiating a hard line with suppliers, or explaining the consequences of late payments to slow paying customers. Besides working with accounts payable and accounts receivable, she also handled insurance claims and organized the company's first personnel department. Dot died in 1975.

While the daughters and granddaughter of Mr. P.A. worked in the office, the grandsons started on the factory floor during summer vacations from high school. "The Boys" (who still carry that label in 1995 though all are in their 60's and 70's) did not enjoy any special privileges handed down by their fathers and mothers. The other employees of Perley A. Thomas Car Works were not asked to treat The Boys as anything special—and they did not. The plant superintendents made it a point to test the Thomas boys to see if they had the same grit their parents had.

Jim Thomas, Norman's son, first started working for the company when he was 16 years old. His job was hand sanding the primer coat of paint on the sides of school buses to create good adhesion for the second coat. At the end of the day he would be coated in dry paint. He longed for the day when another job on the assembly line would open. He got his chance as a member of the pre-drill crew.

Bill Price, the son of Melva Thomas Price and brother to Dot, got his first job in 1938 running a punch press. In the summer of 1939 he worked at night on a three-man rivet crew. During the summer of 1940-41 he kept payroll records for employees in the plant.

John W. Thomas, Jr., the son of Willard, went to work in 1943 sweeping floors and "bucking" rivets, a tedious and noisy job of putting the tip on the rivet then "swelling" it to the right size. His manufacturing crew included a number of women, High Point's version of "Rosie The Riveter," the mythical female factory worker the nation depended on to keep manufacturing humming while the men were fighting. One day John was drilling holes in one of the mobile repair facilities when he carelessly loosened his grip on the drill. It leaped from his hand and the spinning bit dug deeply into his leg. While the scar remains 50 years later, the bigger sting remains hearing the taunts of fellow workers that he was better at drilling his leg than he was at sheet metal.

Albert, son of Norman, was said to be one of the best rivet drivers the company had, despite his youth. Riveters work in three person crews. One person, a "sticker," puts the rivet in the hole, a second drives from the outside and a third person, a "bucker" on the inside, holds a bar of metal against the hole to flatten the rivet once it pops through. The other two men in Albert's crew found it difficult to keep up with him.

The baby of the boys was Pat. Pat launched his career with the company in the bus seat installation position, working with the same man who took great enjoyment from taking the "learner's" percent of his piece pay rate ticket every summer for three years. Pat later moved to the stretch press, a machine which still plays an important role in the manufacture of Thomas Built buses.

The grandsons enjoyed seeing and working with their grandfather as they were growing up. They all share a memory of him that seems amazing for this archon of transportation. Mr. P.A., designer of some of the best streetcars in the world and founder of what would become one of the nation's largest school bus manufacturing operations, was a terrible driver.

The grandsons do not recall Mr. P.A. ever being involved in any serious accidents, but they all remember that he habitually did not pay attention to the road while driving his immaculately maintained and tuned cars. His own sons, Willard and Norman, would walk to work or catch a streetcar rather than ride with him. His problem was not a lack of coordination in controlling the vehicles, but a lack of concentration when he was behind the wheel. Sometimes he would lose himself in deep thought solving a design problem. Other times he would be too closely listening to the conversation of his passengers. Whatever the situation, he would sometimes forget what he was doing and cruise through a red light or forget to stop to let someone out of the car.

A teenaged friend of Bill Price once accepted a ride from Mr. P.A. without knowing the driver was Bill's grandfather. The boy leaped from the car when Mr. P.A. did not stop at the agreed-upon destination. The boy thought he was being kidnaped when Mr. P.A., thinking about work, had simply forgotten the teenager was in the car with him.

One other habit The Boys associate with their grandfather, a lifelong cigar smoker, was that he was constantly, if softly, clearing his throat. More than once a designer would jump when he would hear a soft cough in his ear as Mr. P.A. would be peering over the man's shoulder at some drawing.

During the 1950's The Boys did not see Mr. P.A. often as he had divorced their grandmother Margaret and moved to Jacksonville, Florida. When the company faced any thorny design issues, his sons would ask him to fulfill his consulting contract with the company. Mr. P.A. was so dedicated to his design work that he would not even bother leaving the factory at the end of the day. He would simply share a trailer on the property with a security guard.

Mr. P.A. died at home in Jacksonville in 1958 of heart failure at the age of 84.

As the late 1940's turned into the 1950's, Willard, Norman, Melva and Mary faced what the management of every company realizes after years of slow, steady growth. A market restricted in geographic size is soon saturated. Once that happens the market begins to evaporate. They knew that for their company to grow, they had to expand out of the Carolinas, a strategy Willard had suggested for some time.

While it is a basic principle of any manufacturing business today, setting up a national distribution market for school buses was a new idea in that era. Until that time, school buses had been manufactured and sold only in regional markets. The company competed with as many as five other bus manufacturers in the two Carolinas. It had never ventured into other states. By the same token, Northern-based manufacturers were content to sell in their own larger regions, leaving the Carolina manufacturers to fight among themselves. There were then more than 20 manufacturers of school buses in the nation.

Establishing a national distribution system was essential to the long term survival of the company. To do that A.S. Priddy was hired as the company's first national sales manager. Priddy established a relationship with Pennsylvania sales agents Paul Murray and his assistant Stuart Danner. Other distributorships in Virginia, Maryland, Delaware, Florida, Mississippi, Alabama, and New Jersey soon followed. Succeeding sales managers like James T. Vance helped convince school administrators all along the East Coast to buy buses from a company with a funny name (Perley A. Thomas Car Works) manufactured in a town not easily located on a map (High Point, North Carolina).

The northern-based bus manufacturers did not appreciate this little upstart company from North Carolina muscling in on their territory. One story the Thomas family tells is the time they finally convinced a long-term prospect from New York state to visit the High Point factory so they could demonstrate the quality that went into the company's product. When the prospect had finished the plant tour, the man was amazed that the plant was as modern as it was. Willard and Norman were puzzled by his reaction and asked him why he was so startled.

They learned that other school bus manufacturers had been describing Thomas workers as uneducated hicks who did not know how to build safe buses. The man had been told that the entire Thomas factory was little more than a barn with dirt floors and that the employees worked in their bare feet.

While the story both amused and angered the Thomas family, it also gave them a critical piece of information. Their competitors were worried about them. When competitors worry, you are doing something right.

The Thomas reputation grew so much so fast that a salesman in Canada called in 1960 asking to sell Thomas school bus bodies. John Jr., the national sales manager, worked on the problem of shipping chassis from Canada to High Point then shipping them back with a Thomas body. He found the result to be too expensive. Manufacturing in Canada was a better option. The man invited John for a two-week tour of Canada visiting potential Thomas distributors. As a result of promises extracted from these potential distributors, with board approval, John purchased an existing plant. Working at night using his engineering background, John laid out a production line in that plant. The resulting 100,000-square foot Thomas Built Buses of Canada Ltd. plant opened in 1962 in Woodstock, Ontario.

Some ten years later it was discovered that the title to the facility had never been transferred to the company. That oversight was corrected immediately.

The profitable Canadian venture was further evidence that the second generation of the Thomas family was slowly turning over decisions to the third generation. While John was technically only the national sales manager reporting to the executive committee of his father, uncle and two aunts, all four "seniors" listened to his ideas and agreed to open the plant.

All of "The Boys" sought out similar areas of expertise. Bill Price, who started with the company full time after World War II by delivering buses to customers, discovered a market that would prove profitable in the future. He went to a bus trade show and came back with an order for more than $800 worth of spare parts, a large enough order to prove to "the old folks" that the replacement parts market was almost inexhaustible. Willard and Norman told Bill from that trip on that he was responsible for creating the company's replacement parts business.

Bill was always on the lookout for new product lines that would take the company beyond its traditional markets. One day he followed an old Thomas school bus that appeared to be loaded with boxes. The traditional school bus had been sold to a chicken processor that had removed the seats to load it with cages of baby chicks being transported from the hatchery to grow-out farms.

Bill drove back to the factory and put the company's designers to work. They turned the windows inside out so they could be opened from the outside. A false floor was put in to provide more air circulation to keep the chicks cooler in the summer. The official "Thomas Chick Bus" was on the market within weeks after Bill's encounter with the old school bus. Bill worked from 1947 until retiring in 1987 as vice president in charge of parts and specialty sales.

Albert Thomas found his niche in purchasing by developing an early version of "just-in-time" parts delivery long before it became a management buzz word. He also organized Thomas steel needs so the company could go directly to the mills for the type, quality and quantity of rolled steel the company needed. At the time, all of the other bus manufacturers were buying their materials from warehouse middlemen. Thomas

A Thomas Chick Bus used for transporting small chicks to chicken farmers. The windows were turned inside out so a driver could open and close them from the outside.

was one of the first companies to use the cost efficiencies of bypassing the warehouses to buy direct from the mill.

Jim Thomas had never given much thought to working for the company. After a stint in the U.S. Navy, he returned to North Carolina State University to get an industrial engineering degree with the idea of finding work with a major ship builder. He had already accepted a job with the Norfolk Naval Ship Yard when his father Norman talked him into at least trying the company business. He agreed to start in plant operations in 1957.

Though trained to be an engineer, Jim found that he liked labor relations best of any of his duties. The factory had been forced to admit the United Auto Workers Union in the 1940's as part of an agreement to bid federal government contracts. Jim's goal was to show the company's workers that they did not need the union. He helped develop a retirement plan, improved health benefits, and saw to it that line workers could approach management directly rather than being forced to go through a shop steward. The employees voted the union out in 1960. The vote was not even close.

Jim Thomas retired in 1991 as executive vice president with responsibilities over engineering, production, chassis manufacturing and human resources

Pat Thomas assumed responsibility for the parts department using his experience as a Naval supply officer. His father Willard passed him responsibility for government sales. Government sales were important to the company due to the seasonality of school bus production. Government orders often filled out periods of slow business.

Pat established Perley A. Thomas Car Works as an international company. As early as 1958 he traveled to Mexico, Central and South America looking for dealers. Pat opened two South American factories in Ecuador and Peru in the 1960's (later closing them when those markets declined due to those nations' economic problems). He developed "boxed body" shipments that took Thomas Built buses to worldwide markets. His knowledge and expertise in the export markets led to his appointment as chairman of the North Carolina Ports Authority. Pat was serving as Vice President of International Operations and Commercial Sales when he retired in 1991.

John Willard Thomas Jr. first thought he wanted to be a chemical engineer instead of a bus manufacturer. He pursued that degree at Virginia Polytechnic Institute before switching over to industrial engineering. He spent his early years with the company making wooden models of buses and working in the pattern shop. Later, as National Sales Manager, he further developed the company's national distribution and sales network. He would later serve as company president.

Willard, Norman and Melva treated their children like any other employees. John once went to his father with the plea that he was making only $62.50 a week, which was not enough to support his wife and small son. Willard nodded and agreed to give him a raise. The next week, John Jr., son of the company president, saw that his pay had been increased to $65 a week.

It was the lure of higher pay that came with sales commissions that took John Jr. to the role of national sales and marketing director. He and cousin Bill Price persuaded the family to put them on commission for selling buses and bus parts. That worked better than any of the parties had hoped. The boys thought they were growing rich until the day Willard came into their offices after examining salary records. He told them that he and Norman would not put up with the fact that two young salesmen were making more money than the president and vice president of the company. By the end of the week John and Bill were back on straight salary.

When Willard died in his sleep of a heart attack in 1972 at age 71, Norman was named president of the company. Norman served as president for more than a year before his nephew, John, assumed the job.

John and all the other grandsons of Mr. P.A. were ready to return Perley A. Thomas Car Works to the national consciousness as a major transportation company.

By 1964 the word about Perley A. Thomas Car Works buses was spreading. This bus went to Mississippi.

Chapter 7

Thomas Built Buses Set the Standard

Following the death of Willard in 1972, the retirement of Melva that same year (she died in 1991), and the retirement of Norman in 1973, the third generation of the Thomas family, "The Boys," were in charge. It was a period of shakeout and consolidation in the bus manufacturing industry. For more than 50 years, the industry had been locally and regionally focused. Virtually every state in the nation had its own bus body manufacturers and more than 20 companies were trying to establish national reputations.

For years there had been room for small companies, but during the 1970's the federal government became involved with school bus safety. Demands were made upon manufacturers to make the buses safer while still keeping them at low cost to the school districts. Smaller manufacturers, unable to cope with new specification requirements, began to fold or merge into larger companies.

Thomas had always tried to add safety features within the bounds of the bid specifications. The company found itself growing stronger as the government mandated everything; better frames and brakes, more warning lights, mirrors, emergency exits and a floor structure and side walls that would not buckle in a collision. When the government mandated new safety standards or equipment, Thomas was able to comply and still build buses at a profit while many of its competitors could not. One of those that never became a competitor on the national scene was the company that had informed the state of North Carolina in 1936 that Perley A. Thomas Car Works did not have the wooden frames it needed to fulfill the state's bid specifications.

The new leadership formally changed the name of the company in 1972 to one more in keeping with its product line. What had been Perley A. Thomas Car Works now became Thomas Built Buses, Inc.

1972 was also the year the family first explored the idea of an initial public offering that would put Thomas Built Buses' stock on the market. The Thomas family had serious misgivings about putting their company on the stock market, because they had always maintained a discrete silence about the company's financials. At the time they felt they had little choice. The company founded by a single man had subdivided itself through the years until there were 137 shareholders, all members of the family by blood or marriage. Not all of the shareholders worked for the company, and selling shares was difficult to do since there was no realistic or equitable way to value those shares.

After the experience of working with Willard's estate, some family members worried that liquidity problems would only increase as time passed and the company continued to prosper. On top of that, federal estate laws are written to favor the government, almost requiring that a company be sold off piecemeal by succeeding heirs in order to raise money to pay estate taxes.

Solving the problem was postponed when the country entered a recession in 1972 causing the market for public offerings to dry up. While the initial public offering did not take place, the atmosphere of the company changed in anticipation that something of like manner would be taking place in the near future.

Even though Thomas Built Buses was still a family business, the third generation began to make changes to operate more like the major corporation it had become. The board of directors was expanded and outside directors with no family connection were invited to join. Outside consultants were brought in to evaluate everything from office procedures to manufacturing expectations. A more formalized corporate officer structure with specific duties was created. Formal annual reports were written and distributed to all of the family stockholders. Younger stockholders were encouraged to attend the annual meeting to ask questions about their ownership in the company.

In 1985 consultants offered the family three choices: a complete sell-out to a competitor; another initial public offering; or a management buyout with willing, employed family members staying with the company with other family members selling their stock to a third party.

Selling out to a competitor when the company was healthy had no appeal at all to the family members. The family had built the company from the ground up and they did not want the Thomas name to be erased. The initial public offering was not attractive because the family would have to fully disclose traditionally guarded financial and sales information. That information would be used by the competition, none of which were public companies.

Management buyout had the most appeal. The third generation still liked the bus business and the fourth generation was beginning to participate in the company just as their fathers had done. In 1985 John Thomas Jr., Jim Thomas, Bill Price, Pat Thomas and Albert Thomas joined with three non-family members (W.P. Duncan, treasurer, Morris Adams, vice president of marketing, and Roger Chilton, vice president of sales) to form the nucleus of a management buyout of the company. Providing the impetus to buy out the remaining family members was a New York City-based investment group called Odyssey Partners. Today, in 1995, Odyssey Partners has an equity position in the company while members of the Thomas family remain in the lead management positions.

In early 1992 John W. Thomas Jr. turned over the duties as president of the company to John W. Thomas, III, called "J3" by Thomas employees. Chris Thomas, another son of John Jr., is fleet sales manager/contract sales. Doug Harrison, vice president of manufacturing, is married to Susan, the daughter of Jim Thomas. Bob Price, Bill's son, is national sales manager. Bradley Thomas, Albert's son, is responsible for purchasing in the chassis department.

As of 1995, John Jr. remains chairman of the board and chief executive officer. Pat and Jim remain board members, though both have retired from active management.

While the competition to win bus contracts remains just as fierce as ever, the number of competitors has dropped to just four major companies in 1995. Today, Thomas has 34 percent of the market. Bluebird Bus Company of Ft. Valley, Georgia, has approximately 33 percent. Carpenter Bus Company of Mitchell, Indiana, has 11 percent, and Amtran of Conway, Arkansas, has 9 percent. Other small bus manufacturers maintain the remaining 13 percent.

Thomas Built Buses executives expect their company will change as the market dictates with continuous additions being made to the product line, as well as regular expansion and

Four generations of Thomas's and four out of five of the company's presidents (1951). From left to right—John Thomas Jr. (holding second-born son, Michael A. Thomas), John W. Thomas III (boy standing), J. Willard Thomas, and Perley A. Thomas.

improvements that will be made at all three plants in North Carolina, Canada and Mexico.

The exact future cannot be predicted. As with most manufacturers, product and design changes in one year can dramatically affect what happens in the years that follow. For example, in the 1950's, the company decided to develop a non-conventional bus for use in crowded cities. That led to the development of the engine-forward chassis to eliminate the engine cowling so the driver could better see in front of the vehicle. That early design later led to several increasingly better rear-engined chassis designs. Those newer chassis designs found their way into a variety of products for both school and commercial markets.

New products also mean new technology. In 1993 a Thomas Built bus powered by natural gas was driven cross-country on a 35-day, 3,500-mile road trip from North Carolina to California to demonstrate that the technology and refueling stations were already in place. Powered by a 5.6 liter natural gas engine, the bus has a 300-mile range.

This natural gas powered bus is designed to operate in crowded major cities where exhaust fumes are a problem.

In late 1994 Thomas unveiled its electric, battery-powered bus for use in densely populated urban areas where exhaust gas emissions are a problem.

The bus, called "Sparky" by employees, has a range of up to 60 miles. While no orders had been accepted for the bus as of early 1995, Thomas Built is patiently continuing to develop the model. Company officials are confident the Thomas Electric will soon be in production.

No customer need escapes the engineers at Thomas Built Buses. Several years ago they noted the trend in young moth-

This electric battery powered bus was introduced in 1994.

ers returning to school. The company developed the MOMS (Mobile Occupant Mini Seat), a child safety seat that could be safely strapped into a bus seat.

Children in wheelchairs are easily hoisted aboard a Thomas Built bus equipped for the service and then rolled into a safe position where the wheelchairs can be secured to the floor. Thomas pioneered the design of buses to accept wheelchair lifts not as an add-on, but as an integral part of bus design. At the same time company designers were developing a quality lift, they were working to include a wheelchair escape ramp under the rear emergency door, all in the continuing design tradition of Mr. P.A.

No design detail is too small for Thomas Built Buses. Several years ago Thomas Built introduced a safety latch that prevents the entrance doors from being accidentally opened. The same latch prevents the doors from being opened at night by vandals. Other models have been modified to raise the level of the floor above the wheel well, ending the problem of those unlucky children who had to ride "over the hump."

The company continues to look for new markets in which to promote its products. In early 1995 the company announced plans to build a bus manufacturing plant in Mexico. That will mark a reentry into the Latin American market as the company once had two factories operating in South America.

Thomas Built Buses has built a long lasting reputation. After 60 years building buses, the company estimates it has sold more than 300,000 units all over the world. It is among North Carolina's top 20 exporters. In 1993 exports increased 44 percent over 1992.

In 1995 Thomas Built Buses produced more than 8,000 buses a year in High Point and another 2,500 in Canada. The High Point operation covers more than 184 acres in seven buildings with 686,000 square feet under roof, while the Canadian operation is in two plants covering 225,000 square feet on 60 acres. Together the two operations employ more than 1,500 people. Thomas is the largest industrial employer in High Point.

For the past five years, total annual production for both the United States and the Canadian operations has topped 10,000 units. Daily production has grown from one bus per day to 36 per day in High Point, 18 per day in Canada, and four per day in Mexico.

In 1994 the company was awarded the largest single contract in its history, a $104 million bid to manufacture 2,000 buses for the South Carolina school system.

Thomas Built Buses has come a long way since Perley A. Thomas agreed to enclose some summer streetcars.

Chapter 8

To Build a Bus

It is not hard to imagine what it is like inside the Thomas Built Buses factory in High Point. It is noisy. Holes are being drilled through sheet metal. Wheel wells are being sawed out of other pieces of sheet metal. The top caps of buses are being stretch-formed. More than a thousand people are moving around one huge building.

There are 64 stations in the Thomas Built factory with a schedule of moving each bus to the next station every twelve and a half minutes.

The bus floor starts as a flat sheet of steel with two raised areas that will become the wheel wells. Steel bow frames are welded on the outside of the floor with several inches of the frame extending below the floor. While most other bus manufacturers do not extend their bow frames below the level of the floor, Thomas Built Buses has determined that these extensions act as a barrier, keeping smaller vehicles from running underneath a bus.

Once the frames are welded in place, the front and rear caps are welded onto the bus. The frame, now mounted on roller wheels which ride rails placed on the floor of the factory,

Saf-T-Liner®-ER™
84 passenger School
coach with Thomas
chassis

Chartour Commercial
Coach

Citiliner City Transit
Coach

Thirty-six buses a day roll out of the Thomas Built Buses factory.

Inside the High Point factory

is pushed to another assembly station. This station is where the side walls are riveted in place and the steel for the wheel well is cut away. The bus body is beginning to take shape.

As the body advances through the factory, plywood is placed over the floor for sound deadening and insulation. More insulation is added to the sides and ceiling, even inside the bow frames if the bus is destined for delivery to a school district in a cold climate.

Once the body has been insulated and windows installed, it is ready to be lifted onto one of several styles of chassis. Thomas Built Buses has been building its own rear-engined chassis since 1977 and its own front-engined chassis since October 1994. The diesel engines from Cummins or Caterpillar come in four different horsepower ratings, depending on what part of the country the bus will operate. Conventional chassis are manufactured by Navistar or Ford and are delivered daily to the Thomas Built factory.

Once the bus body and the chassis have been bolted together, the bus then rolls forward into a large painting booth where the familiar yellow paint is applied. Once the paint is dry, the stop signs, warning lights and other safety devices are added to the bus.

Seats, also manufactured by Thomas Built, are added to the bus at this point. The seat frames are welded by robotic machines, the only aspect of the assembly operation that is not performed by human workers. Once the seats are added and a final inspection made, the buses are then driven to another Thomas site where final preparation such as painting the name of the school district is completed. Once the bus is complete, school districts either send their own drivers or hire a "drive away" company to deliver the bus to its final destination.

The manufacturing of a single bus, from start to finish, from first weld to final sweeping of the inside, takes about two weeks. The production schedule in early 1995 called for the completion of 36 buses every day working on a single shift, five-day week in High Point. The Canadian plant produces 18 buses per day.

The company has kept several manufacturing practices from the days when streetcars were built on the same site as today's modern factory. Once the day's goal has been met, the employees are free to leave, giving them an incentive to work quickly and efficiently. Haste does not lead to waste, however. Each department inspects its own work, meaning that at least 64 inspections of each bus are completed before it leaves the factory. Every employee is trained in at least one other job so if one part of the production line is short due to illness or vacation, other employees can fill in so manufacturing is not slowed.

Chapter 9

Seeing Thomas Streetcars Today

It is easy to find Thomas Built buses on the road. There are tens of thousands of them transporting millions of children to school every weekday. Still more thousands are on duty on military bases, with county and state penal institutions, and with city transit systems. Other Thomas Built buses move airline passengers from the airport to car rental agencies. Still others transport small groups on field trips.

Thomas Built buses can be seen every day all over the country. Perley A. Thomas streetcars can be seen in only a few select places.

New Orleans is the only city in the United States still running conventional streetcars. Streetcars first were introduced in the city in 1835 when the New Orleans and Carrollton Railroad first began operation with steam engines pulling a few cars from downtown New Orleans to the resort town of Carrollton. After the Civil War, former Confederate General P. G. T. Beauregard revived the line using horses or mules to draw the cars.

The horsecars lasted until 1893 when the first electric powered cars, built by the St. Louis Car Company, went into opera-

The New Orleans streetcars used to feature advertising. Note the $20 fare from New Orleans to Houston. (From Joe Bell collection)

tion. Later, these cars were replaced with Southern Car Company streetcars designed by Perley A. Thomas. The streetcar lines underwent a major reorganization in 1922 when the New Orleans Public Service took over all operations of the streetcars within the city. In 1923 and 1924 the utility completely modernized its lines, including buying 98 Perley A. Thomas Car Works Series 800 and 900 streetcars. In 1928 New Orleans ordered ten 1000 series streetcars. (All of the New Orleans streetcars running today are from the 800 series.)

These Perley A. Thomas streetcars ran for nearly 10 years before New Orleans joined the national movement to buses. It took more than 30 years for almost all of the streetcars to be replaced by buses. By 1964 only the St. Charles line was still running. Eleven of the street cars that had been running on the Canal Street Line were sold to trolley museums around the country.

By 1984 interest for revitalizing the city's streetcars lines, both as tourist attractions and for public transit, had grown to the point that citizens formed committees to bring back the streetcars. At first, the city proposed using new facsimiles of Perley A. Thomas streetcars. The public demanded real Perley A. Thomas streetcars, the same ones that had been running in the city for 60 years. The Regional Transit Authority restored its original streetcars at less cost than it would have been to buy new streetcars that looked like old streetcars.

The city even tried to buy back the streetcars it had sold more than 20 years earlier. Three of the 11 sold away in 1964 were purchased and restored in 1985 for operation on the Riverfront Line, New Orleans' first new streetcar line since 1926. In 1988 all of the 35 streetcars owned by the city underwent a $10.2 million face lift, part of a total $47 million renovation of the entire streetcar system that included replacing track, cross ties, rock ballast and modernizing the streetcar maintenance barn.

The most popular of the city's two streetcar lines is the St. Charles Street line, which runs a 13.2 mile crescent from Candelet St. at Canal Street in the city's downtown business district through the city's most majestic neighborhoods. The line passes preserved pre-Civil War homes, historic monuments, Loyola University, Tulane University, the Audubon Zoological Gardens and dozens of restaurants and hotels before reaching the end of the line at Carrollton Avenue. Then the seats are reversed, the front and rear power poles are switched and the car returns to the business district. A streetcar regularly passes a given point on the line within 10 minutes.

Much of the track runs on what is called "neutral ground" between the streets. The streetcar track is recessed in the ground with the cross ties buried several inches below the surface. Grass grows right up to the rails, giving the impression that the streetcars are gliding across a well-kept lawn. The ride is smooth. Any sideways movement or jostling is an indication

Bruce Thomas, great-grandson of Perley A. Thomas with Federal Transit Administrator, Brian Clymer marking the opening of Carrollton, Louisiana Car Barn used for refurbishing P.A. Thomas streetcars. (January 1992). Bruce is VP of Marketing for Digital Recorders, Inc., a supplier to the transit industry. Car #937 is an original Perley A. Thomas Streetcar.

that the ties below the surface have deteriorated and should be replaced.

Streetcar service on the St. Charles line is available in New Orleans 24 hours a day, every day of the year. A one-way trip takes about 45 minutes with a round trip taking just over an hour and a half. Although the cars are rated to have a top speed of around 27 miles per hour, stops are frequently made so the average speed is around 15 miles per hour. More than 20,000 commuters and visitors use the line daily. More than six million people ride the city's streetcars each year with some tourists just riding the 1.9 mile Riverfront line along the Mississippi River that links various developments with the French Quarter. The Riverfront line is served by four Perley A. Thomas Series 900 cars painted red and yellow to resemble the colors of the cars that ran decades earlier in the French Quarter. The cars are known locally as "The Ladies In Red."

One fact borne out by the popularity of New Orleans streetcars is that they are just as economical, if not more so, than the city's diesel buses. The New Orleans Regional Transit Authority once compared the two modes of transportation and found that streetcars cost 28 cents per mile to operate compared with 34 cents per mile for buses. Maintenance costs were 68 cents per mile for a streetcar and 66 cents for a bus. A streetcar carries an average of nine passengers per mile compared to an average of six per mile for a bus.

New Orleans' streetcars are 47 feet, eight inches long; seven feet 10 inches wide; and 11 feet, four inches tall. They weigh 42,000 pounds. Each is a double truck (two sets of wheel assemblies) at each end of the car. Two 65 horsepower motors, operating at 600 volts and 93 revolutions per minute are located over each set of trucks. They are painted a dark green with red trim. The seats, once made of cherry or sometimes rattan, are now all mahogany. They are handbuilt by the carpenters at the Carrollton car barn.

The New Orleans' Perley A. Thomas cars will forever be famous with drama and movie lovers. In 1947 Tennessee Williams set his tragic play "A Streetcar Named Desire" in New Orleans. The play was named after one of the St. Charles line streetcar stops along Desire Street.

Another operating Perley A. Thomas streetcar is owned by the Midwest Electric Railway Association in Mt. Pleasant, Iowa. This car (Number 381 but originally known as Car 379) was one of 10 streetcars built for the Knoxville Power and Light Company in 1930. It is 39 feet, four inches long, eight feet, five inches wide, and 10 feet, seven inches tall. It weighs 32,500 pounds and seats 44 passengers.

Knoxville sold three of its cars to the Waterloo, Cedar Falls and Northern Railway in 1947 for use in service between downtown Cedar Falls and Waterloo, Iowa. One of the cars was destroyed by fire in 1949 and the second by fire in 1954. The last car was retired from service in 1958. It was the last streetcar to operate in Iowa in regular service and was acquired by the Association in 1973. The streetcar is operating as part of the Annual Old Threshers Reunion for the five days ending each Memorial Day. Car 381 is taken from the car barn along with seven other streetcars and used in a regular transit service along a 1.5 mile track. The Midwest Electric Railway Museum is on Threshers Road, Mount Pleasant, Iowa 52641(phone 319-385-8937). In a touch of irony, this Perley A. Thomas streetcar makes its run near the manufacturing plant of Bluebird Bus Company, a competitor to Thomas Built Buses.

The following museums all have Perley A. Thomas Streetcars. All were bought from New Orleans in 1964 when the city closed its Canal Street line:

The Waterloo, Cedar Falls and Northern Railway car that runs every Memorial Day weekend in Mt. Pleasant, Iowa. This streetcar originally ran in Knoxville, Tenn. (R. Wesley Bender photo)

The largest museum is the Seashore Trolley Museum, also called The Museum of Mass Transit, at 195 Log Cabin Road, Kennebunkport, Maine 04046 (telephone 207-967-2712). This museum has over 150 exhibits, including Car Number 966 from New Orleans, which makes occasional runs for visitors.

Branford Electric Railroad, also called the Shore Line Trolley Museum at 17 River Street, East Haven, CT 06512, (telephone 203-467-6927) has more than 80 exhibits, including Perley A. Thomas Car Number 850 from New Orleans.

Connecticut Electric Railway Association, also called the Connecticut Trolley Museum at Box 360, East Windsor, CT 06088 (telephone 203-627-6540) has 58 exhibits, including Perley A. Thomas Number 836 from New Orleans.

Pennsylvania Trolley Museum, operated by the Pennsylvania Railway Museum Association at One Museum Road, Washington, Penn. 15301 (telephone 412-228-9256) has 38 exhibits, including Car Number 832 from New Orleans.

The Orange Empire Railroad Museum at Box 548, Perris, CA 92570 (Phone 909-943-3020) has 157 exhibits, including Car Number 913 from New Orleans.

The North Carolina Transportation History Museum at Box 44, Spencer, North Carolina (telephone 704-636-2889) has an unrestored Thomas streetcar (Car number 918) from New Orleans.

The Chattanooga Choo-Choo Hotel in Chattanooga, Tennessee operates another New Orleans Car, Number 913, on a short track behind the hotel.

Charlotte Trolley, P.O. Box 35434, Charlotte, NC 28234 on South Blvd. near downtown Charlotte has restored a streetcar built by Southern Public Utilities (today's Duke Power Company) that is a virtual copy of the 1924 Perley A. Thomas streetcar built for New Orleans. The Charlotte Trolley was the last streetcar to operate in the city and now runs on weekends along a short line ending in the trolley barn. There are long range plans to restore the old trolley tracks to uptown Charlotte. At that time The Charlotte Trolley would become a symbol for the return of light rail to the city. The museum is located near the intersection of South and East Boulevards, in the Dilworth neighborhood. Dilworth was Charlotte's first "streetcar suburb."

From Rails . . .

(R. Wesley Bender collections)

To Roads

AFTERWORD

Contributions of Thomas Built Buses to Charity and Community

written by Thomas S. Haggai, Chairman and CEO, IGA

In 1956. moving to the city of High Point, I realized I had come to a city that was an industrial dynamo. It was the same year the String and Splinter was organized as a businessman's club... the "string," signifying our hosiery and the "splinters," for our furniture. High Point, which at that time was producing about sixty percent of men's hosiery and about an equal amount of women's, was on its way to its present status where eighty percent of all furniture sales originate at the semi-annual international markets held here.

However, I soon learned there was a "rest of the story." The vibrancy of our city came from a balance between these two prominent industries created by other non-related companies led by what we now know as Thomas Built Buses.

Almost within a few days of living in the city I simultaneously met two brothers, J. Willard Thomas and J. Norman Thomas, the second generation of leadership of Thomas Built Buses, along with their sister. Norman, his wife Mary and son James were faithful attendees at the church where I was senior minister. I met Willard again when asked to join the board of the YMCA. In both cases, almost instantly, I realized that generosity was not something either of these brothers claimed, but both of them exemplified. Never once did I talk with Norman Thomas about giving, but he became one of the top three givers of our church and looked for opportunities to give more. The budget of the YMCA and the spending of the YMCA at that time had no relationship. It was always in the red. Each month, upon hearing the negative report, we'd be balanced by the personal generosity of Willard Thomas and his sidekick, A. Pat Brown.

As an aside, there is an interesting story about Perley A. Thomas and A. Pat Brown. Perley A. Thomas, during the latter years of his life, had lived at the Sheraton Hotel in High Point, also the home of Pat Brown. It was there one night, when they were having a drink and a smoke together, that Perley was complaining that the demand for streetcars was diminishing and he couldn't have one optimistic thought about his company. Then the rather soft-hearted but gruff-sounding Pat Brown literally cursed him out, calling him everything he could think of that was insulting saying, "With your brain, why don't you realize it is over and start building some other (@#&^!+$!) means of transportation. This may have had as much influence upon Perley Thomas making a decision to get into building school buses as any other.

A company is nothing more than the extension of its leadership, and from that moment in 1956, now forty years later, there has not been a worthy cause in High Point for which Thomas Built Buses has not been the leader in giving. In the majority of instances, the company has given even before solicitation. The Thomases have believed that stewardship begins with the assurance that their employees were adequately paid and recognized. Closely following was a sense of "corporate rent" to the city where they were headquartered. This was through supporting eleemosynary causes that give character to a community.

The inside chuckle for any of us involved in fundraising was: "Will we be able to deliver our proposal to Thomas before we receive their check?" Now some companies give quickly to protect the size of their gift. My experience with Thomas was that we often received more from the company than we might have proposed. I'm not speaking of token gifts either, as evidenced by the $500,000 given to High Point Regional Hospital during just one of its many campaigns. The list of recipients Thomas Built Buses' charity is long and covers a broad range. (See the list which follows.)

John Thomas started on a local level helping his own five sons in the Boy Scouts of America, all of whom went on to become Eagle Scouts. The same aggressive leadership he gave as president of the company caused Scouting to recruit him—first to Council President, then to Regional President and to the National Board and international Scouting, and most recently as National Commissioner, chairing along the way most significant committees as a member of what many consider to be the most prestigious volunteer board in the country.

Chairman John is not alone in matching his time with his gifts. Cousin Jim Thomas quietly accepts committee roles of basic institutions. Brother Pat literally led the North Carolina Port Authority into the modern world, significantly impacting our state's world business. Our jammed soccer fields are a tribute to John Thomas III, now corporate president.

What gives added meaning to their giving is that few companies have given as many dollars with as little recognition as Thomas Built Buses. There is nothing improper about enlightened self-interest. In fact, any student of the Bible realizes that all the giving suggested in the Bible has some "self" involved, in such terms as "tithe in order that the windows of Heaven might be opened," or "give so you may be given to." Thomas Built Buses has never turned their giving over to their public relations department. They have very carefully examined the worth of each cause. When a cause was refused, it was because it did not fit their very broad profile. Thomas Built Buses has given first priority to the city where they've had their headquarters, but they have not put geographic boundaries on their generosities. Their corporate giving is the reflection of the individual giving of each of the executives.

In the four decades I have watched closely the corporations of our city, serving for a decade as chairman of our CEO Roundtable (no connection with any other business groups but a distinctive force of twenty-four corporate leaders and an ad hoc planning mode for our area), Thomas Built Buses would receive the award for their attitude and their range, both in value and spread of their contributions to society.

In 1995 they set a new record for any High Point area corporation in their United Way contributions. This is a barometer. Many of us believe the best way to measure the effectiveness of your company's morale is to check the United Way giving. Without arm-twisting or unusual pressure, they exceeded their goal.

Isn't it ironic to find that something as sturdy, mechanical and heavy as a bus is produced by a company with such a tender heart? This may be an added reason to have confidence that such a company would be extremely dedicated to the safety of the thousands upon thousands of children whose journey to and from school every day depends upon those yellow Thomas Built Buses.

Below is a list of recipients of contributions from Thomas Built Buses:

Alcoholics Home, Inc.

Allen Jay Middle School

American Humanics

American Red Cross

Archdale-Trinity Band Boosters

Archdale/Trinity YMCA

Big Brothers & Big Sisters

Bishop McGinnis High School

Boy Scouts of America

Boys & Girls Club

Business & Professional Men's Club

Carl Chavis YMCA

Catawba College

Cities in Schools

Delta Sigma Theta Sorority, Inc.

Dr. Jerry D. Paschal Memorial Scholarship

Eastern Music Festival

Furniture City Classic

Gradfest

Heartstrides

High Point Arts Council

High Point Parks & Recreation

High Point Regional Hospital

High Point Soccer Association

High Point University

High Point University Humanics

I CARE, INC.

Independent College Fund of NC, Inc.

Kiwanis Boys & Girls

March of Dimes

Maryfield Nursing Home

Meals-On-Wheels

N. C. Association of School Resources

North Carolina Amateur Sports

North Carolina Citizens for Business & industry

Oak Hill School

Old North State Council-BSA

Summer Economics Institute-UNC Greensboro

The Piedmont School

The Salvation Army

Theater Art Galleries

United Way of Greater High Point

Urban Ministry of High Point

Wallburg Boosters Club

Wesleyan Transportation Ministry

Westchester Academy

Winston-Salem/Piedmont Triad Symphony

Valued Contributors to the Success of

Perley A. Thomas Car Works and Thomas Built Buses, Inc.

The Thomas family recognizes that thousands of employees of Perley A. Thomas Car Works and Thomas Built Buses, and other people around the country have contributed to the business success they have enjoyed over the past 80 years. The following are some of the many people who helped this company in its early formative years. We thank those listed and every person who has made Thomas Built Buses what it is today:

Morris Adams–Vice President Sales & Marketing

Ralph Albert–Chief Industrial Engineer

Archie Allred–Engineer

Harold "Chip" Aulbert–Plant Engineer

Larry Bannon–Vice President-International

Guillermo Benjamin–Central American Regional Sales Manager

Benno Bodenhorst–Manager Carrocerias Ecuatorianas, S.A.

C.C. Brown–Director of Student Transportation for NC Dept. of Education

Roger Chilton–Vice President Sales & Marketing

Ted Clayton–Vice President-Sales & Marketing

Jim Cole–Plant Superintendent in High Point and Canada

Stuart Danner–Distributor for Pennsylvania

Terry Dawson–Plant Engineer

Lee DeLano–Government Sales/Ford

W.P. "Buddy" Duncan–Treasurer/Chief Financial Officer

John Everhardt–Upholstery Supervisor

F.H. Goins–Purchasing Agent

Carroll Eugene "Fats" Graham–Regional Sales Manager for Tennessee

Harry Halker–Steel Mill Supervisor

Iris Horner–Office Manager

Jerome Hutchens–Skilled Wood Craftsman

Paul Justice–Canadian Plant Superintendent

Hernan R. Leroux–South American Regional Sales Manager

Matt Mathison–Engineer/Department Supervisor

Charles McConkey–Vice President Human Resources

Larry McSwain–Industrial Engineer

Paul Murray–Distributor in Pennsylvania

Wesley Pickle–Transportation Supervisor for Tennessee Dept. of Education

A.S. Priddy–Sales Manager

Bill Purser–Manager Chassis Division

Nelson Sales–Delivery Supervisor

Harry Saunders–Production Manager

Chris Schultheiss–Plant Supervisor

Clarence Schultheiss–Plant Superintendent

Gilbert Scott–Engineer/Designer

Art Shipwash–Paint Foreman

Clayner Shipwash–Electrical Foreman

Don Spencer–Steel Mill Supervisor

Floyd Teed–Automotive Engineer

Arnold Thingstad–Government Sales/General Motors Corporation

Ralph Thornton–Maintenance Supervisor

Louis "June" Trexler–Project Engineer

Jim Tydings–Engineer/Department Supervisor

Beth Umberger–Export Secretary

J.T. Vance–Vice President-Sales & Marketing

Dennis "Sarge" Walker–Production Support Supervisor

Raymond Wimbish–Transportation Supervisor for Virginia Dept. of Education

Jim Wrenn–Superintendent